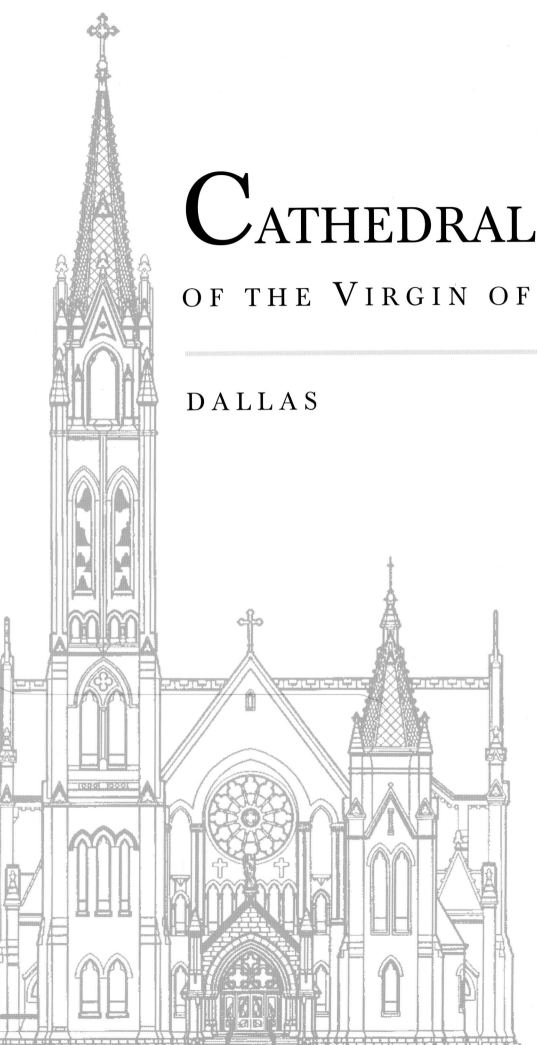

# CATHEDRAL SHRINE

## OF THE VIRGIN OF GUADALUPE

### DALLAS

STEVE LANDREGAN

PRODUCED IN COLLABORATION
WITH THE CATHEDRAL RESTORATION
AND PRESERVATION FUND

**Publisher**

**Éditions du Signe**

**B.P. 94 - 67038 Strasbourg, France**

Publishing Director

**Christian Riehl**

Director of Publication

**Joëlle Bernhard**

Author

**Steve Landregan**

Research

**Joyce Higgins**

Design and Layout

**Sylvie Tusinski**

Photography

**Frantisek Zvardon**

Photoengraving 106942

**Atelier du Signe**

Copyright Design and Layout

© Éditions du Signe, 2006

ISBN 10: 2-7468-1712-8

ISBN 13: 978-2-7468-1712-8

Printed in China by Sung Fung

# Beloved Friends

I greet you in the name of this venerable Cathedral that was dedicated over 100 years ago to the Sacred Heart of Jesus.

We are grateful to our ancestors who loved Jesus, sought to build a community in His name, strove to be faithful disciples and worked hard to build a church that would forever proclaim his message of love.

This Cathedral has been a beacon of hope for many as they migrated to the southwest United States seeking a better life and the Sacraments of the Church. They were also seeking a faith community to which they could connect in an enduring way and establish a long-lasting legacy.

In more recent years, the Cathedral was put under the care of Our Lady of Guadalupe and was rededicated as Catedral Santuario de Guadalupe. Since that time, it has been embraced by a diverse community that continues to manifest the rich tapestry that makes up the Tradition of the Catholic Church.

The Cathedral is one step nearer completion as the towers and bells are finished, and the renovation of the building is bringing it back to its original luster. It towers over the entire City of Dallas as a beacon of God's love and our hope for His continued care for all our people.

The Cathedral stands as a powerful sign in the city of Dallas that the Catholic presence is alive and well and will remain so for generations.

Sincerely,

Most Rev. Charles V. Grahmann. D.D.
Bishop of Dallas

# Cathedral Rectors

Hundreds of priests, deacons and women religious have ministered at the Cathedral parish since its founding in 1873. They have given, and continue to give of themselves unselfishly to tend this corner of the Lord's vineyard. We have been enriched by their ministries of service.

THE FOLLOWING PRIESTS HAVE SERVED AS RECTOR, PASTOR OR ADMINISTRATOR OF SACRED HEART CHURCH, SACRED HEART CATHEDRAL OR THE CATHEDRAL SHRINE OF THE VIRGIN OF GUADALUPE.

| | | | | |
|---|---|---|---|---|
| Rev. | Mathurin Pairier | Pastor | 1873 | 1874 |
| Msgr. | Joseph Martiniere | Pastor | 1874 | 1888 |
| Msgr. | Joseph Blum | Pastor/Rector | 1890 | 1897 |
| Rev. | Jeoffrey Hartnett | Rector | 1897 | 1899 |
| Rev. | John Hayes | Rector | 1899 | 1908 |
| Msgr. | J.S. O'Connor | Administrator | 1908 | 1911 |
| Msgr. | Bernard Diamond | Rector | 1911 | 1941 |
| Msgr. | Augustine Danglmayr | Rector | 1941 | 1942 |
| Msgr. | W.J. Bender | Rector | 1942 | 1948 |
| Msgr. | John Gulczynski | Rector | 1948 | 1952 |
| Msgr. | William O'Brien | Rector | 1952 | 1961 |
| Msgr. | Thomas Tschoepe | Rector | 1961 | 1965 |
| Rev. | Sebastian Valles, OCD | Rector | 1965 | 1966 |
| Rev. | Denis Lynch, OCD | Rector | 1966 | 1969 |
| Rev. | Patrick Ahern, OCD | Rector | 1969 | 1972 |
| Rev. | Andrew Palermo, OCD | Rector | 1972 | 1974 |
| Rev. | Jenaro de la Cruz, OCD | Rector | 1974 | 1987 |
| Rev. | Felix Da Prato, OCD | Rector | 1987 | 1988 |
| Msgr. | Lawrence Pichard | Rector | 1988 | 1999 |
| Rev. | Ramón Alvarez | Rector | 1999 | 2006 |
| Rev. | Eduardo González | Rector | 2006 | |

THE FOLLOWING COMMUNITIES OF WOMEN RELIGIOUS HAVE SERVED THE CATHEDRAL PARISH SINCE ITS ESTABLISHMENT.

Daughters of Charity of St. Vincent de Paul
Missionary Catechists of Divine Providence
Missionary Catechists of the Poor
School Sisters of Notre Dame
Ursuline Nuns

# Past is Prologue

History is a story of stories and historians are no more than storytellers.

There are two stories to tell about Dallas' Cathedral Shrine of the Virgin of Guadalupe; both are stories of growth and change. One is the story of the Cathedral itself, the towering structure in the center of Dallas' Arts District that took 103 years to complete. The other is the story of a vibrant Christian community, the largest cathedral congregation in the United States, whose earliest members were among the first settlers of Dallas.

*"Standing Room Only" is the norm at most Sunday Masses at the Cathedral which has the largest Cathedral congregation in the nation and an average Sunday attendance of 11,500 worshippers.*

The home of Maxim Guillot, a French immigrant carriage maker, was the site of the first Catholic Mass of record in Dallas.

In 1856 Bishop Jean Marie Odin, first Bishop of Galveston, sent his Vicar General, Monsignor Louis Chambodut to Dallas to make contact with the La Reunion colonists.

Interestingly the beginnings of the present Cathedral go back to three years before the Diocese of Dallas was established by Pope Leo XIII, when in 1887 Father Joseph Martiniere, who was pastor of Sacred Heart Church, contacted Texas pioneer architect Nicholas Clayton about designing a "cathedral" for Dallas.

Among those who found their way to the village of Dallas, established by John Neely Bryan in 1841, were likely a few Catholics, but their identities and names are lost in the mists of time. The first Catholic of record was Maxim Guillot, a French immigrant carriage maker who set up shop in Dallas in 1852 after moving from Fort Worth.

Of course, the two stories are actually one. The Cathedral itself is nothing more than the physical expression of the Faith, hopes and dreams of the men and women, prelates and priests who have sacrificed to create this temple of worship on their journey to God.

Most historical accounts of the beginnings of Catholicism in Dallas report that Father Sebastian Augagneur, a French missionary from Nacogdoches, celebrated the first Mass in 1859 in the home of Maxime Guillot. But there are indications that there were earlier stirrings of the Faith. In the Diocese of Dallas archives there is a notation in the records of Sacred Heart Church that the Catholics in Dallas were first ministered to by Father Michael Sheehan, a priest of the Diocese of Galveston, who was a fulltime Army Chaplain at Fort Belknap in Young County. Army records show that Father Sheehan did indeed serve as a chaplain at Fort Belknap from 1855 to 1859.

Further indications of Catholic presence in Dallas are related to the establishment in 1855 of La Reunion, a utopian commune, across the Trinity composed of 200 French-speaking artisans, followers of French democratic socialist and atheist François Fourier.

Word of the colony reached Bishop Jean Marie Odin, who's Diocese of Galveston embraced all of Texas. In a letter to Rome in 1856, he spoke of his "great desire to consider the means of bringing them back to the practice of their [religious] duties," and sent his Vicar General, Father Louis Chambodut, to visit the colony.

Father Chambodut was familiar with the area having earlier spent five-years, from 1846 to 1851, ministering to isolated Catholics from the mother church of Northeastern Texas in Nacogdoches. During his two-month journey in 1855 or 1856 Father Chambodut visited Dallas and reported that presence of seven "Catholic Anglo families" who were eager to have a church and a priest.

*Father Louis Chambodut was apparently the first priest to visit Dallas in 1856 and reported finding seven Catholic families.*

Nevertheless it was not until 1859 that we have an historical record of the first celebration of Mass in Dallas. The year Father Augagneur celebrated Mass in the Guillot home for the family and two single men identified only as Carey and Walsh.

French priests from Nacogdoches continued to visit Dallas periodically to minister to the small

*Father Thomas Hennessy, an Irish immigrant, was one of the several " circuit rider" priests who visited Dallas from Nacogdoches.*

*Father Joseph Martiniere, who rode circuit to Dallas from Nacogdoches, established the first permanent mission station in North Texas at St. Paul in Collin County, and served Dallas Catholics from there.*

Catholic community. Among them, in addition to Father Augagneur, were Father Claude Neraz, the future first Bishop of San Antonio, Father Thomas Hennessy an Irish immigrant from Henrietta, Texas, who became a priest after his wife died in child-birth and Fathers Joseph and Claude Martiniere, blood brothers.

In 1868 a mission station from Nacogdoches was established at St. Paul community in Collin County, where a number of Irish Catholic families had settled and built the first Catholic Church in the area. Father Joseph Martiniere was assigned to St. Paul from where he served Dallas and other North Texas communities by horseback.

John Neely Bryan's tiny village had changed drama-tically. Dallas was enjoying phenomenal growth. In 1868 the first steamboat arrived in Dallas after navigating the Trinity River from Galveston sparking never-to-be-realized hopes that the city might become a river port. A year later Dallas received its first "piped in" water from Browder Springs and by 1870 the federal census recorded a population of 2,960. A new charter in 1871 officially made Dallas a city a step up from a town.

In this bird's eye view of Dallas in 1872, provided by the Dallas Historical Society, the location of the original Sacred Heart Pro-Cathedral is indicated 1 and the site of the present Cathedral 2. The original Pro-Cathedral was located at the side of the Old Post Office at what is now St. Paul and Bryan Sts. At that time St. Paul was called Masten and Federal was called Cottage Lane.

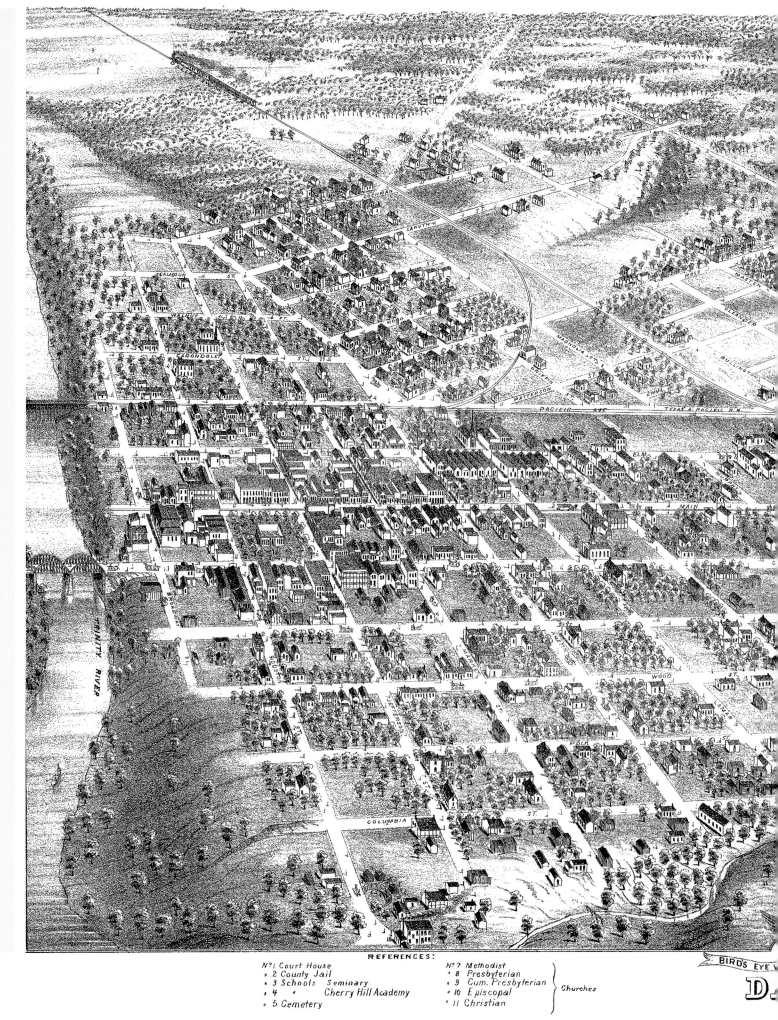

REFERENCES:

Nº1 Court House
" 2 County Jail
" 3 Schools    Seminary
" 4    "    Cherry Hill Academy
" 5 Cemetery

Nº7 Methodist
" 8 Presbyterian
" 9 Cum. Presbyterian    } Churches
" 10 Episcopal
" 11 Christian

BIRDS EYE V

D

OF THE CITY OF

AS

REFERENCES:

12 H. & T. C. R. R. Depot
13 T. & P. " " "
14 D. & W. " " "
15 I. O. O. F. Hall
16 Masonic "

17 Post Office
18 City Mills
19 Dallas Herald
20 " News
21 Breweries

Drawn by H. Brosius.

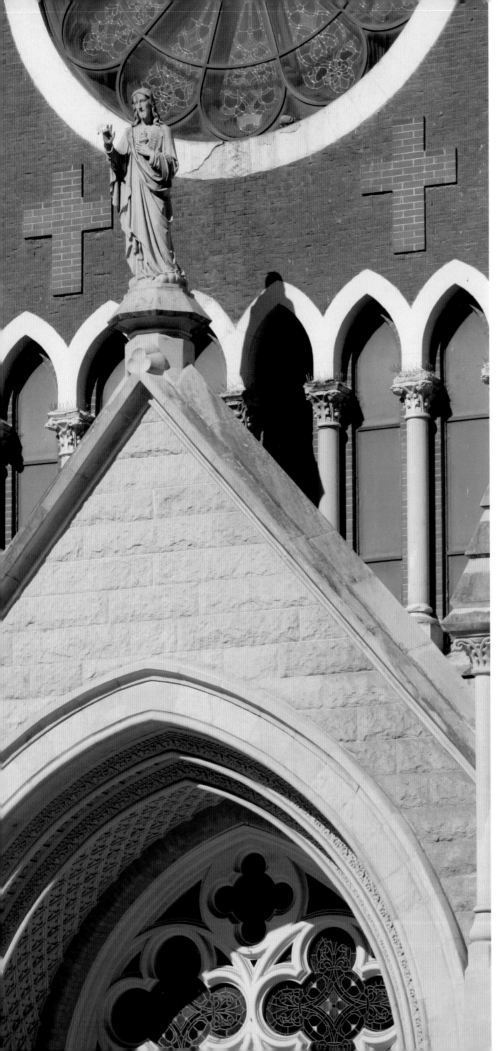

A statue of the Sacred Heart, the patron of the Diocese of Dallas, stands atop the front entrance to the Cathedral.

Because of the availability of coastal steamers and riverboats for fast transportation early settlement in Texas had been along the Gulf Coast and the Red River. The coming of the railroads soon changed that and the enterprising citizens of Dallas found ways to attract the railroads to the city. In 1872 the Houston and Texas Central Railroad arrived from the South bringing with it railroad workers and railhead merchants. In 1873 the Texas and Pacific Railroad arrived from the East making Dallas a cross-roads with direct connections to all parts of the nation. Many of the new arrivals, particularly the Irish railroad workers, were Catholics.

Restoration of the Cathedral has returned the walls to the pristine white of the original structure. Renovation work has provided a new magnificent hardwood floor in the sanctuary. The new altar carved in Pietrasantra, Italy, rests on four pedestals, each of three columns representing the Trinity. The total of twelve columns represents the Apostles. A carving of grapes and wheat sheaves is etched into the top of each column symbolizing the Blessed Sacrament.

# Beginnings

In 1872 Bishop Claude Dubuis, who succeeded Bishop Odin when Odin had been made Archbishop of New Orleans, established the first parish in Dallas under the direction of Father Mathurin Pairier a veteran missionary who came to Texas after serving in Australia. For a year the Dallas community met at the Odd Fellows Hall for Mass on Sunday. In 1873 a lot was purchased for $500 dollars on the corner of Bryan and Masten [now St. Paul] and a small frame church was constructed. The church was dedicated on the First Sunday of August in 1873.

In a history of the Dallas diocese written in 1908 by Father (later Bishop) Joseph Patrick Lynch, he tells of how Henry Harrington, an early parishioner told of how at the Odd Fellows Hall, "One Sunday at Mass Father Pairier announced they were going to build a church and that after Mass they would vote on the choice of a name. 'I want the church called The Sacred Heart of Jesus,' Father said. Harrington laughed and added 'after Mass all of us Irish boys voted for St. Patrick, but, of course, the women voted with the priest and the church was named Sacred Heart.'"

*Sacred Heart Church, predecessor to the Cathedral, was established in 1872 by Bishop Claude Dubuis, second Bishop of Galveston.*

*Standing on the site of the Old Post Office at St. Paul and Bryan, the first frame church was built in 1872 under Father Mathurin Pairier, the first pastor.*

IN MEMORY OF
JAMES MORONEY

*This sketch from the Ursuline Archives, shows the first convent for the Ursuline Nuns who came to Dallas in 1874 to open the Cathedral School. The small frame building also served as the school until an additional structure was completed.*

Father Lynch lists among the families belonging to the parish at that time Guillots, Blakeneys, Rogers, Barrys, Bricks, Cullens, Cabells, Davises, Hogans, Clarks, Kanes, Walshes, Kings, Smiths, Matthews, Hoes, Burkes, Moroneys and Taltys.

Before the church was completed Father Martiniere replaced Father Pairier as pastor of Sacred Heart. Wanting to expand the parish property Father Martiniere purchased a cotton patch, the balance of the block upon which the church had been built. To his surprise he found that the price was $3,700 dollars, $3,200 more than the same size lot a year earlier. The coming of the railroads had changed everything. Records show the property was sold in 1900 for $40,000 and it was purchased for the Post Office Site 20 years later for $200,000.

A school and convent were built on the new property and the Ursuline nuns opened Sacred Heart School on February 2, 1874 with seven pupils. The Ursuline nuns came from Ursuline Academy in Galveston. At the request of Father Martiniere and Bishop Dubuis the Galveston community agreed to send six Ursulines to Dallas to establish the school. It was necessary to make an addition to the combination convent/school building before the end of the year.

*Schoolboys gather in the yard of the two story frame building that was the first Cathedral school when completed in 1874.*

By 1875 there were 128 pupils and a new two-story building was constructed. The Ursulines also took over a boy's school on Wood Street taught by a Mr. Martin Quinn. That school would become the parish school for St. Patrick's parish in 1882. That same year the cornerstone was laid for Ursuline Academy, which was completed in 1884. When the academy opened the nuns continued to teach at Sacred Heart School.

*Boys and girls were enrolled in Ursuline Academy when it opened in 1878, but the classes were soon restricted to girls and young women. Mother St. Paul, left, and Mother Evangelista are pictured on the Academy steps with their young students.*

*Ursuline Academy, designed by Nicholas Clayton who was also architect of the Cathedral, was one of the most magnificent structures in Dallas during the 1880s and 1890s.*

Dallas continued to grow. The first iron bridge over the Trinity was built in 1872, the first streetcars (mule driven of course) were introduced in 1873, gaslights were installed downtown and gas mains served most neighborhoods in 1874. Because of the financial panic of 1873 the T & P Railroad had to temporarily cease construction and Dallas became the railhead. It was the height of the tragic slaughter of buffalo to the west and Dallas became buffalo hide market of the world.

*In 1890, Bishop Nicholas Gallagher, asked that his large Diocese of Galveston be divided and Pope Leo XIII established the Diocese of Dallas on July 15, 1890.*

Because of the railroads, Dallas was rapidly becoming a major city. The first telephone was installed in 1879 and by 1881 there were 40 subscribers. The Dallas Morning News began publishing in 1885 and the first traffic ticket was issued for driving a horse too fast on Main Street. The fine was $1. By 1890 Dallas became (for the first and only time) the largest city in Texas with a population of 38,067.

As the number of Sacred Heart parishioners increased, Bishop Nicholas Gallagher, administrator of the Diocese of Galveston, established a second parish in Dallas. Mr. Harrington's "Irish boys" from 1873 got their wish. The new church was named St. Patrick and Father Vitalus Quinon, who was an assistant at Sacred Heart, was named pastor. A new frame church was built on Cabell Street between Pearl and Preston, on land donated by the Houston and Texas Central Railroad.

When the Diocese of Galveston was established in 1847 it embraced the entire state. In 1874 The Diocese of San Antonio was established with former Dallas missionary Father Claude Neraz as first bishop. A short time later the Vicariate Apostolic of Brownsville was established. By 1890 Bishop Gallagher recognized that he no longer could administer the burgeoning northern portion of the state from Galveston and petitioned that a new diocese be established.

# Foundations

In personal scribbled notes in the possession of the Catholic Archives of Texas Bishop Gallagher wrote: "The Diocese of Galveston is too large to be conveniently and promptly attended from Galveston, which is at the southern extremity of the Diocese, so that some parts of the Diocese are at least 800 miles distant, (although in that portion as yet there are few Catholics still the prospect is that portion will soon be settled.) The N. of Texas is grow[ing] fast in pop. and material prosperity, and the good of the Church and religion will be subserved by having a Bishop located there whe[re] he can conveniently look after the interest of Catholics."

*Pope Leo XIII, (Gioaccino Pecci), who erected the Diocese of Dallas, followed closely the expansion of Catholicism in the United States and the colonial world.*

After consultation with the Archbishop of New Orleans and other bishops of the province, Pope Leo XIII was asked to establish the Diocese of Dallas. On July 15, 1890 the Pope issued a bull stating in part: "...giving attention to the facts put forth by the Bishops of the Province of New Orleans... we divide and separate our Diocese of Galveston by the power of this document and with the fullness of Apostolic Power... and by the same authority, we erect a Diocese with the name of Dallas, named after the city of Dallas, in which we establish the See of the Bishop, which city has the greatest population and two churches..."

Interestingly the bull did not designate a cathedral church so it was left up to the first bishop to make that choice between Sacred Heart and Saint Patrick churches. It was not until April of 1891 that the new bishop arrived. He was Thomas Francis Brennan, an Irish born clergyman who was brought to America as a child by his widowed mother. He received a classical education in the United States and Europe and became a priest of the Diocese of Erie, Pennsylvania. Bishop Brennan made Sacred Heart Church

*Bishop Thomas Francis Brennan was named First Bishop of Dallas by Pope Leo XIII*

his Pro-Cathedral or temporary cathedral presumably because it was the first and oldest parish in the city.

On April 26, 1891, the *Dallas Morning* News reported that "Right Rev. Dr. Thomas Brennan, the first bishop of Dallas arrived in the city yesterday from Galveston. He was met at Miller's on the Central by a committee consisting of Fathers Blum and Brickley and Messers James Moroney, T. F. McEnnis, Hugh Blekeney, Tom King and Michael Coerver..."

*"Prairie Gothic" would aptly describe the interior décor of Sacred Heart Cathedral, Dallas' first or pro-Cathedral.*

It was obvious that a cathedral was high on the new bishop's agenda. The *Dallas Herald* noted that, "Bishop Brennan, the new Catholic bishop of the diocese, arrived in Dallas last evening and was given a warm welcome by the Catholic clergy and laymen of the city. Bishop Brennan will begin work at once on the new cathedral and other institutions."

In an interview with a Dallas Morning News reporter the new bishop said "The greatest effort I wish to make now is to get the new cathedral of the Sacred Heart on a solid basis. We are all beginning new and I hope that the people of Dallas will take hold and build the cathedral, which is very necessary." Then taking note of the financial crisis then gripping the country he continued "On account of the financial depression that the country is feeling it seems a little difficult to raise ready cash at present, but some of the principal men of the parish were with me this morning and they gave me words of encouragement. The priests of the diocese will meet with me next Tuesday evening and after consulting with them I will know better what to do in all matters."

Reality soon tempered the dreams of the new bishop. Father Lynch describes the situation Brennan actually faced when he assumed the leadership of the new diocese. "In the city of Dallas itself, the Bishop found two frail, wooden structures, the pro-cathedral of the Sacred Heart struggling with a thirty thousand dollar debt, and the newer parish of St. Patrick's. The pro-cathedral, an old frame structure hastily built in 1873, was in bad condition."

Bishop Brennan found himself beset by a conspirancy of circumstances exacerbated by the depression of the 1890s that was shaking the national economy and would not abate until 1897. A major problem was the $30,000 debt owed for the land on which the present Cathedral sits. Father Lynch relates, "...feeling that Dallas should have a representative church, Father Blum, then pastor, had bought a most desirable block of ground located on the corner of Ross and Pearl for thirty thousand dollars, the intention being to pay for the new site by selling the old property at Bryan and Ervay, there being quite a boom in

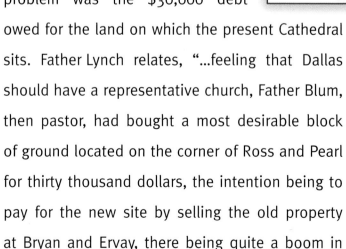

*Father Joseph Blum, pastor of Sacred Heart Church before the diocese was established, had purchased the present Cathedral site for future expansion.*

real estate at this time. Just before the arrival of Bishop Brennan, the boom collapsed, and an embarrassing financial situation settled over the whole city resulting in the financial handicap encountered by the bishop on his arrival."

Bishop Brennan was overwhelmed by his financial problems and a few months after his installation told his priests, "You have spoken of me as a young man; if you want to keep me perpetually young, you will all help in our financial difficulties..."

According to Father Lynch, Bishop Brennan received little help or sympathy, "Though he came to Dallas as a most able man, the situation he met was terribly discouraging to a young prelate. There was no "Extension Society" in existence at that time to aid poverty-stricken diocese or struggling prelates. He had to handle the situation the best he could with what local help he could muster. The laity was embittered because of the financial depression and disappointing reverses. The clergy were divided and even antagonistic."

Frustrated over the financial problems he inherited; in July of 1891 Bishop Brennan chastised Bishop Gallagher for allowing the situation to develop. "All would be pleasant with us were it not for that Ross Avenue deal. You should have never signed either of the notes for Blum."

Financial problems and other difficulties Bishop Brennan encountered in his short but stormy tenure as Bishop of Dallas resulted in his resignation in 1892 when he traveled to Rome for his Ad Limina visit with Pope Leo XIII. Construction of a cathedral would be left to his successor.

# Realization

Edward Joseph Dunne and Thomas Francis Brennan were born within a few miles of each other in County Tipperary, Ireland but the second Bishop of Dallas, was a very different man than his predecessor. Bishop Dunne was careful, deliberate and determined. He did not have the arrogance and brashness of Bishop Brennan. What they did have in common was the determination to build a cathedral. Bishop Dunne would succeed where Bishop Brennan failed.

*Bishop Edward Joseph Dunne was appointed second Bishop of Dallas in 1893.*

Within a few months of his arrival in Dallas in November of 1893 he began what today would be called the kick-off of his capital campaign. Bishop Dunne himself was the principal campaigner He was indefatigable. Nicholas Clayton was asked to downsize his proposal to make it more affordable. The Catholic Church Extension society, which raises funds to assist struggling parishes and dioceses, was still some 16 years in the future so Bishop Dunne became his own Extension Society. He traveled extensively raising funds for the cathedral construction

*Bishop Dunne declined a Bishop's residence, preferring to direct funds to the new Cathedral. He lived in a room in the rectory which connected the Cathedral to the school.*

When Bishop Dunne came from Chicago he brought with him $35,000 in gifts from his former parishioners and others. He put all $35,000 into the cathedral, plus another $2,000 given to him on his arrival by the Dallas clergy. He saved the cost of an episcopal residence by living in an upstairs room at the Pro-Cathedral rectory. The nation was coming out of the depression of the 1890s; fund raising was still an uphill battle. Father Joseph Blum, frustrated by the fund raising difficulties resigned in 1897. He was succeeded by Father Jeoffrey Hartnett who was the first priest ordained for the Diocese by Bishop Brennan.

Finally, in 1898, ground was broken for the new Sacred Heart Cathedral which had been shorn of its two steeples because of their additional cost. They would be added later, thus completing the cathedral. The truncated structure would have to wait for 103 years for its steeples, but they now grace the larger and smaller towers, completing architect Clayton's planned cathedral. Sadly, Father Hartnett did not survive to see completion. He died of smallpox during an epidemic in Dallas in 1899. He contracted the disease while ministering to a patient at the pest house, who was not a Catholic but had asked for a priest.

*Eight years after the Diocese of Dallas was established, the cornerstone for the present Cathedral was laid by Bishop Dunne on June 17, 1898.*

# Father Jeoffrey Hartnett

Father Jeoffrey Hartnett, whose picture is memorialized in a cathedral window, was the first priest ordained for the newly established Diocese of Dallas. He was ordained July 5, 1891 by Bishop Thomas Brennan who had been in Dallas only a few months.

He died less than nine years later from smallpox contracted while ministering to a woman dying of smallpox in the pest house. Father Hartnett was rector of the Cathedral at the time. When the word came that the dying woman had requested a priest, Dallas was in the midst of a severe snowstorm. Rather than sending one of his assistants, Father Hartnett himself walked through the blizzard to the pest house to administer last rites to the dying woman.

He contracted the dread disease and died on March 7, 1899. Father Hartnett's death drew much attention and he became known as the "martyr priest". The *Dallas Morning News* reported that "No death that has occurred in Dallas for many years has occasioned more general regret than that of (Father) Hartnett."

Like so many of his contemporaries, he immigrated to the United States in 1870 with his family as a child. Father Hartnett was born in Punt, Abbeyfeale, County Limerick, Ireland in 1859 and first lived in New York before his family moved to Texas.

Prior to his death he had served at St. Patrick Church, Dallas, St. Joseph Church, Waxahachie, St. Joseph Church, Ennis and Our Lady of Victory Church, Paris.

# Fulfillment

Dedication of the cathedral on October 26, 1902, was a grand event. A special feature was the presence of more than 1,000 electric lights outlining the vault above the sanctuary. At a time when electricity was still relatively rare, the cathedral lights required so much power that the Power Company requested that they be notified before they were turned on.

In the brilliantly lighted cathedral the beautiful stained glass windows of the 12 Apostles and many saints dazzled those in attendance.

*At the dedication of the Cathedral on October 26, 1902, Bishop Dunne, center, was flanked by, left to right, Msgr. Aloyisius Granger, Bishop Vander Ven of Natchitoches, Louisiana, Msgr. Joseph Martiniere and Msgr. Joseph Blum.*

A special window was dedicated to Father Jeffrey Hartnett, the clergy of the Chicago archdiocese gave a great rose window, sanctuary windows were gifts of the Dallas clergy and John Joseph Williams, first Archbishop of Boston, donated the organ.

*The Cathedral pipe organ was built in 1871 in New York for the Second Presbyterian Church in Elizabeth, New Jersey. The organ was replaced some thirty years later with a new instrument. The organ was then acquired by Archbishop John Williams of Boston and presented as a gift to Bishop Dunne in 1902.*

Cathedral parishioners had memorialized many of the windows, among them names like King, Cullen, Kane, Matthews and Moroney that had been listed among the original parishioners in 1873. The magnificent carved main altar was the gift of Michael Coerver, who was among those meeting the first Bishop upon his arrival. The Bishop's Throne was a gift of Father S. P. McDonnell, one of Bishop Dunne's priest friends from Chicago.

*Clergy of the Archdiocese of Chicago, where Bishop Dunne had served as a pastor, donated the Rose Window above the organ.*

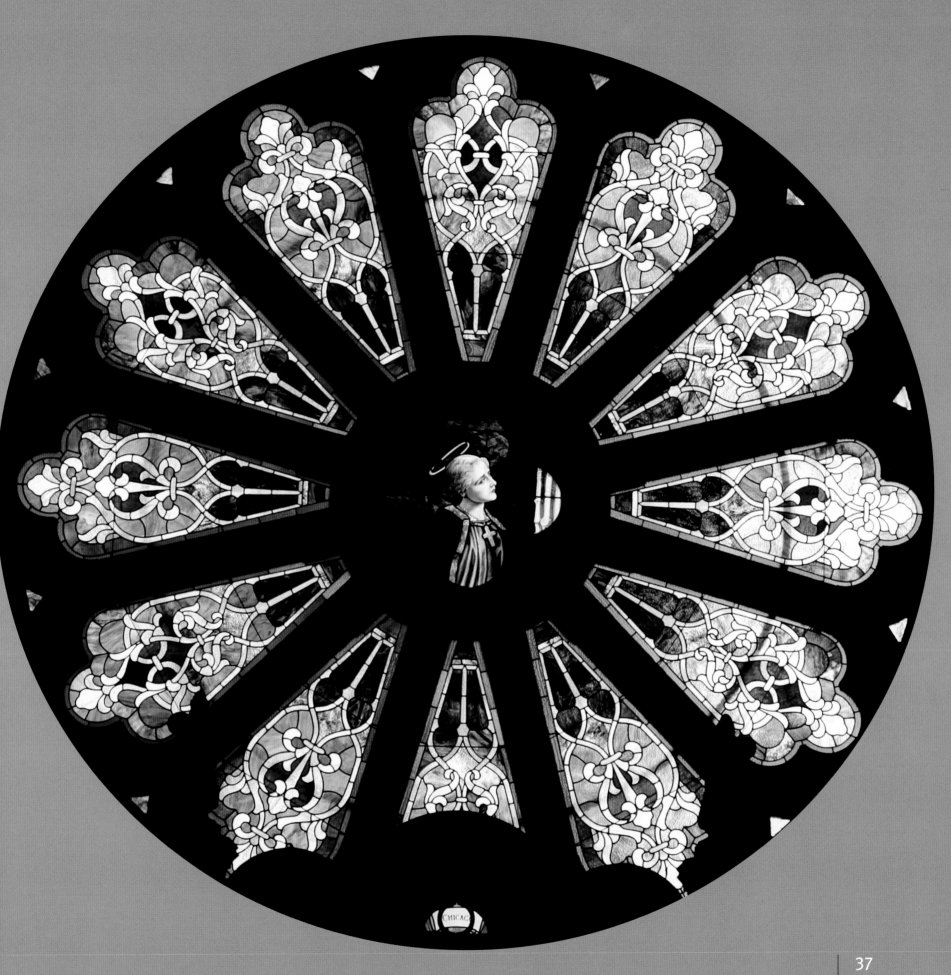

Sanctuary windows above the altar
are from the left:
The Sacred Heart appearing to St. Margaret
Mary Alacoque, St. Bridget,
St. Martin of Tours,
The Assumption of Mary
and St. Patrick.

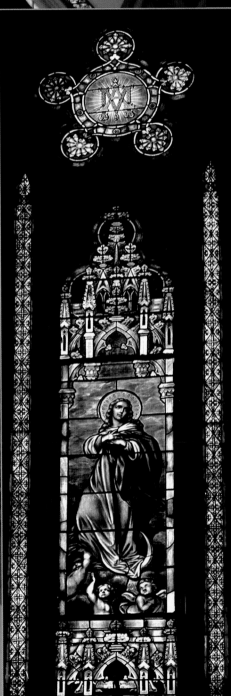

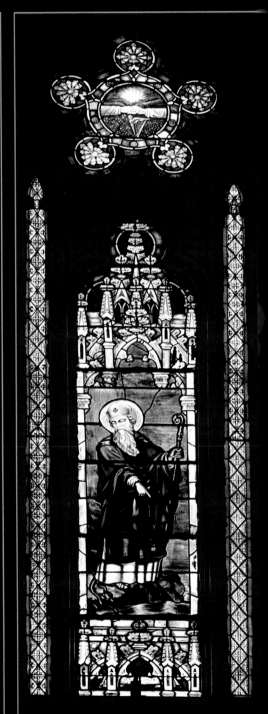

Catholics looked carefully to find their parish window among the 24 donated by churches of the diocese. The Ladies Altar Society had ordered vestments worn by celebrants at the Pontifical Solemn High Mass from France for the occasion and the marble altar rail was a gift of the Ancient Order of Hibernians.

*The Cullen Family, one of the founding families of Sacred Heart Church, memorialized a stained glass window of St. James the Greater, as did many families of the parish.*

Both Dallas newspapers carried full-page coverage of the dedication with pictures and the complete text of the sermons. Visiting prelates and clergy and Catholics from throughout the diocese that extended from Texarkana to El Paso joined in the festivities.

At the Pontifical Solemn High Mass Bishop John Joseph Hennessy, first Bishop of Wichita, Kansas, preached to an overflowing crowd. In the evening, at a second service, Bishop (later Cardinal) John Glennon of St. Louis gave the sermon.

A souvenir booklet featured a drawing of the cathedral (with steeples) on the cover and included photographs of prelates and pastors as well as stories about the cathedral. Included in the souvenir booklet were bio-

*A promise first made by Bishop Brennan upon his arrival was finally fulfilled by his successor twelve years later. This photo was made shortly after the dedication in 1902.*

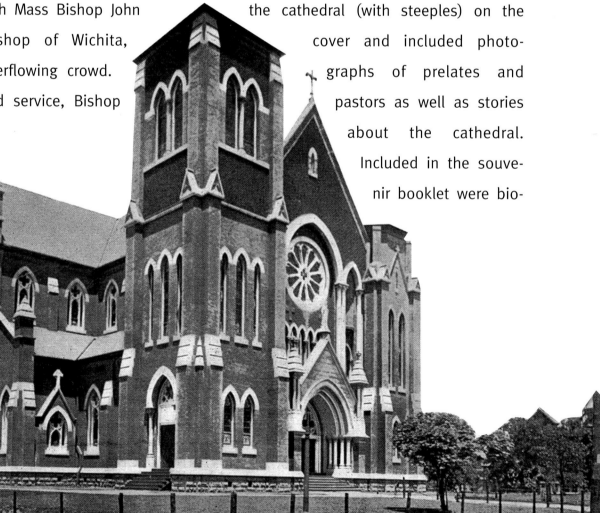

*Parishioners, clergy and religious, including many from around the nation, filled the new Sacred Heart Cathedral in October 1902 for two dedication celebrations, one in the morning and another that night.*

graphies of Bishop Dunne, cathedral pastors and a history of the Sacred Heart Parish. Finally, there was a listing of all parishioners and various items donated for the building and the names of donors. The Cathedral was described as "a stately structure of pure gothic architecture, 104 by 160 feet in size. It is built of pressed brick and stone and when finished will have a large and small tower. Its clerestory is of unusual height, giving the edifice a very imposing appearance. The roof is of tile and all the material used in the construction is of the most substantial character."

The booklet's description was too modest. Clayton's cathedral's interior was a model of beauty and grace with a soaring, hand stenciled 60 foot coffered ceiling, exquisite rose windows and stained glass panels. The domed sanctuary held five altars, one of which was crafted in Italy and installed in 1903. The building was even electrified. Over one thousand incandescent lights studded the walls – one of the earliest uses of electricity in a commercial building in Dallas.

The only thing lacking on October 26, 1902 were the two towers, which the booklet indicated were necessary before the cathedral was finished. It would take 103 years before they would be added.

While the unfulfilled dream of the spires was apparent, Nicholas J. Clayton's Victorian Cathedral had been built. Today, the 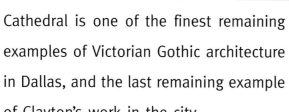 Cathedral is one of the finest remaining examples of Victorian Gothic architecture in Dallas, and the last remaining example of Clayton's work in the city.

43

# Years of Change

Upon the death of Bishop Dunne, Father Lynch, his newly appointed Vicar General was named administrator and was named to succeed Bishop Dunne as Bishop of Dallas in 1911. He immediately appointed Monsignor Bernard Diamond as Vicar General and rector of the Cathedral. Bishop Lynch would serve as ordinary

*Joseph Patrick Lynch, succeeded Bishop Dunne as third Bishop of Dallas upon Dunne's death in 1911.*

*It was a scorching 112° on July 12, 1911, when Bishop Lynch was consecrated and installed as ordinary of the Diocese of Dallas but the heat did not diminish the crowd or it's enthusiasm. Many drove their new horseless carriages to the celebration.*

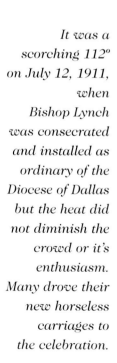

44

of the Dallas diocese for the next 43 years and Monsignor Diamond would continue as rector and Vicar General for 30 years.

Dallas and the Catholic Church settled into a period of lethargy interrupted only briefly by the First World War, a flare up of anti-Catholicism and Ku Klux Klan activity in the 1920s, and the Depression ending only with the beginning of World War II.

The Cathedral was festively decorated with flags and bunting to welcome home the "doughboys" in 1919, a new rectory was built in 1920 and the Cathedral was redecorated in 1925. A Diocesan Synod was held in the Cathedral in 1936 and the Diocese of Dallas gave birth to two daughter dioceses, the Diocese of El Paso in 1912 and the Diocese of Amarillo in 1926. The first Bishop of Amarillo, Bishop Rudolph Gerken, was chosen from the ranks of Dallas clergy.

*Bunting, flags and banners with Bishop Lynch's crest adorned the interior of the Cathedral for his consecration celebration.*

*Flags bedecked the Cathedral and more than 1,000 festival lights sparkled like jewels to welcome the troops home in 1919 after the armistice ending the first World War.*

Y ears of change

With the death of Monsignor Diamond in 1941, Monsignor Wilfred Bender was named Cathedral Rector. In 1947 Monsignor Augustine Danglmayr was named auxiliary bishop and the following year Monsignor John T. Gulczynski was named rector of the Cathedral when Monsignor Bender was named pastor of Christ the King Parish.

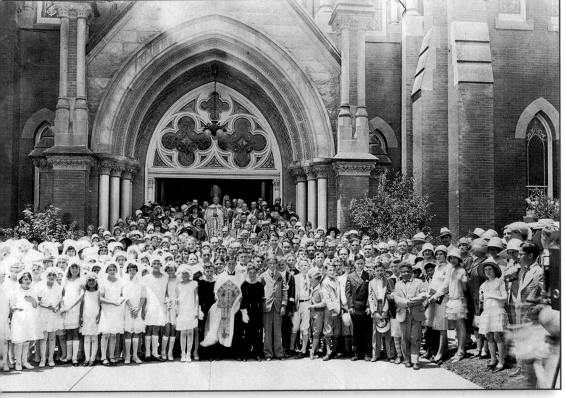

*At 6"5', Bishop Lynch in his tall miter was truly the "Great High Priest" as he towered above the First Communion Class of 1927 on the front steps of the Cathedral.*

*A new school was built behind the Cathedral at Pearl and Flora streets in 1917. The Cathedral Parochial school was closed in 1968 and demolished in 1989.*

The lethargic years ended abruptly for Dallas and the Catholic Church with the Second World War. The war itself brought an influx of defense workers and the end of hostilities resulted in a population boom. In the 10 years between 1930 and 1940 the population of the City of Dallas had increased by a mere 30,000. By 1950 it had increased by another 130,000 and by 1960 by another 250,000 people. Many of the new residents were Catholic and 12 new parishes were established in the 1940s, half of them in the City of Dallas. In 1952 Monsignor Gulczynski was made pastor of the new St. Thomas Aquinas Parish and was replaced as Cathedral rector by Monsignor William F. O'Brien.

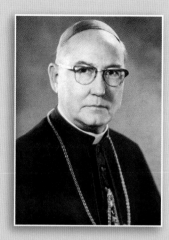

*Monsignor Augustine Danglmayr, Dallas' first auxiliary bishop, was appointed in 1942 to assist Bishop Lynch whose tenure extended 43 years, from 1911 until his death in 1954.*

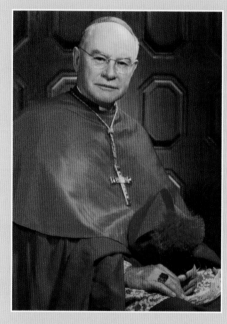

*In 1952 Bishop Thomas Kiely Gorman of Reno was named coadjutor Bishop of Dallas to assist the ill and aging Bishop Lynch in the administration of the growing diocese. He succeeded Bishop Lynch as fourth Bishop of Dallas upon Bishop Lynch's death in 1954.*

Many Catholics were moving to Dallas, but they were moving to new parishes in the suburbs and outlying areas. As a result, the boundaries of the Cathedral were changed and the Cathedral congregation began to shrink. Nine new parishes were established in the Dallas area in the 1950s further diminishing the number of Cathedral parishioners.

Bishop Thomas K. Gorman was made co-adjutor Bishop of Dallas in 1952 and became Bishop of Dallas upon the death of Bishop Lynch in 1954. One of his first actions was to change the name of the diocese to the Diocese of Dallas-Forth Worth and to name St. Patrick's Church in Fort Worth as co-cathedral.

*In this historic photograph, Sacred Heart Cathedral is pictured as it was for many years prior to the Second Vatican Council. The original high altar, fashioned and donated by Michael Coerver, was replaced due to deterioration of the wood and was replaced with a table altar to conform to the liturgical renewal. The picture also shows the festival lights which were part of the original design.*

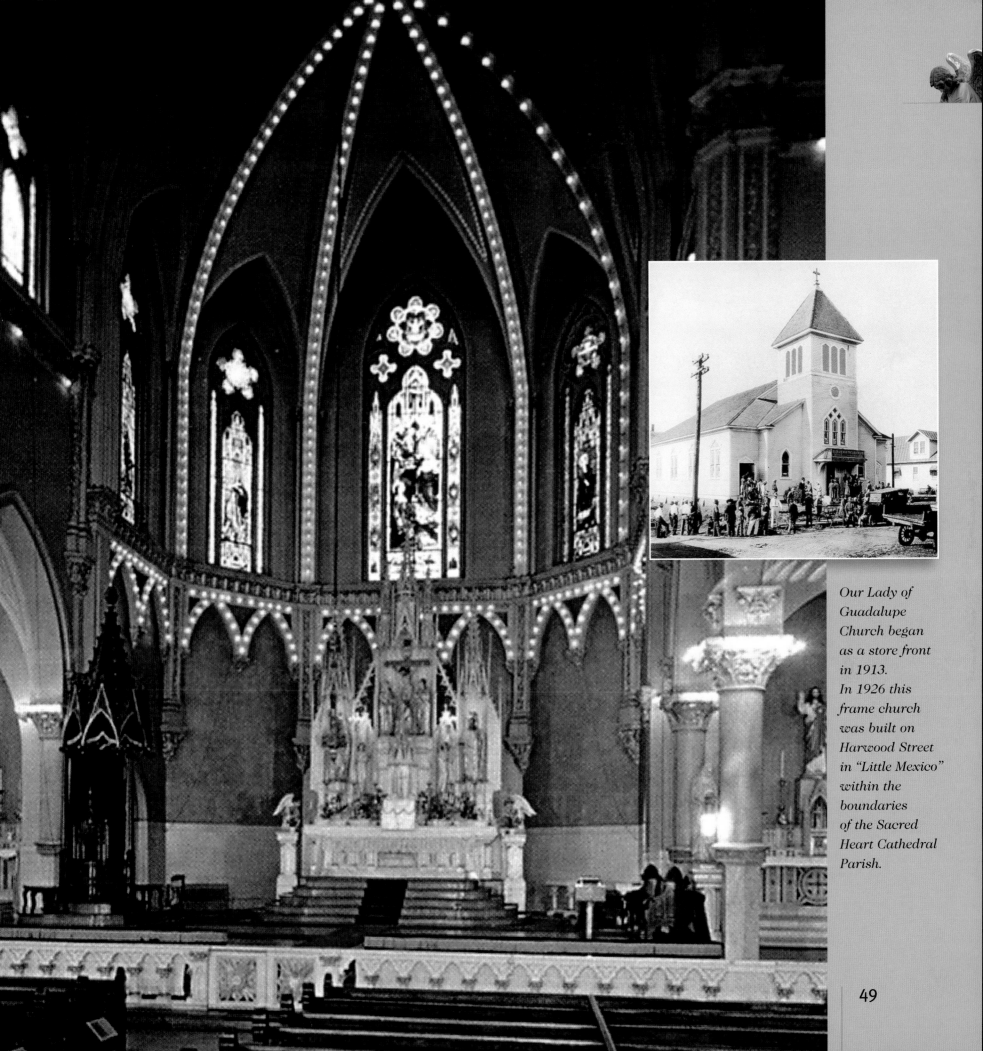

Our Lady of Guadalupe Church began as a store front in 1913. In 1926 this frame church was built on Harwood Street in "Little Mexico" within the boundaries of the Sacred Heart Cathedral Parish.

In 1961 Monsignor Thomas Tschoepe was named rector of the Cathedral. Attendance at Masses on both Sundays and weekdays was pitifully small. Our Lady of Guadalupe Church which was within the Cathedral boundaries, but was considered a national parish, was experiencing the opposite problem. The congregation had long since outgrown the small frame church on Harwood Street and was unable to raise sufficient funds to build a new church.

Bishop Gorman met with the priests and parishioners of Our Lady of Guadalupe and the Cathedral and it was agreed that the two parishes would merge and the Carmelite Fathers, who were in charge of Our Lady of Guadalupe would assume administration of the Cathedral.

In 1969 Bishop Thomas Tschoepe succeeded Bishop Gorman and became the first native-son bishop. He petitioned the Vatican to change the name of the Cathedral from Sacred Heart to Our Lady of Guadalupe an action many of the longtime Cathedral parishioners regretted.

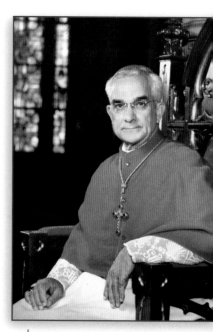

Carmelite Father Sebastian Valles was named rector in 1965 and was replaced by Carmelite Father Denis Lynch in 1966. Mass attendance began to increase but the parochial school was forced to close in 1968 due to decreased attendance. It was a time of both hope and turmoil in the Church in the wake of Vatican II and it fell to Carmelite Father Patrick Ahern, who be-

*Bishop Thomas A. Tschoepe, like Bishop Danglmayr, a native son of the Diocese, was Bishop of San Angelo when he succeeded Bishop Gorman upon his resignation in 1969. He became the fifth Bishop of Dallas.*

*In one of several renovations to accommodate liturgical changes after the Second Vatican Council, the altar was replaced in the center of the sanctuary and a massive carved image of Christ hovered above.*

came rector in 1969, to refurbish the sanctuary to conform to the liturgical changes mandated by the Council.

It was a painful experience to see the ornately carved Main altar removed, but wood rot would have required its removal even without the Council reforms. The *Cathedra*, the Bishop's chair, was refinished in white and placed in the middle of the sanctuary behind the temporary altar and the communion rail was removed. Later a massive wood sculpture of Christ by Heri Bert Bartscht with outstretched arms but no cross was hung above the altar.

In 1974 Carmelite Father Jenaro de la Cruz became rector and held the post for twelve years-time, during which the Vatican approved the Cathedral name change.

*Cabinet maker and craftsman Michael Coerver, a descendent of a founding family, fashioned and donated the great high altar that graced the sanctuary from 1902 until the post Vatican II renovations when deteriorating wood resulted in its destruction.*

The new official name was Cathedral Shrine of the Blessed Virgin Mary of Guadalupe. Most people of course immediately shortened it to Guadalupe Cathedral.

Another sanctuary renovation included the installation of a needlepoint of the image of Our Lady of Guadalupe behind the altar and the moving of the cathedra or bishop's chair to the side. The tapestry was the work of priest-artist Father Bascomb G. Eades, who also designed and executed tapestries for the two side altars. The tapestry of

Our Lady of Guadalupe was 25 feet tall and six feet wide and dominated the Cathedral.

Carmelite Father Felix DaPrato became rector in 1987 after a new contract had been executed with the Carmelites in 1986. Two years later the Carmelites withdrew from the Cathedral and Monsignor Lawrence Pichard a diocesan priest, was named rector.

Bright Realty made a proposal to the diocese that would result in a high rise office building being constructed on the corner of Ross and Crocket streets, where the Cathedral rectory presently stood. The rectory and school were demolished and a monstrous excavation made right next to the Cathedral. During the excavation a weakening of the Cathedral foundation occurred requiring shoring up and repair to prevent damage to the main structure. Bright suffered financial setbacks and construction never started on the high rise office building, but the hole remained.

# Restoration

It was a critical time and there were those who felt the best course of action was to relocate the cathedral to an existing church or build a new one from scratch. After consultation, Bishop Charles Grahmann announced that the Cathedral would stay and should become an integral part of the new Arts District that had grown up around it. The Bishop committed himself to work for the restoration of the Cathedral to its original grandeur.

With a serious commitment to restoration of the Cathedral a committee of parishioners and diocesan personnel began meeting in 1997 to develop a master plan. In October 1997 the Cathedral Restoration and Preservation Fund, Inc., was established for the purpose of raising capital to restore, preserve and renovate the Cathedral. In addition to Bishop Grahmann and Father Ramón Alvarez, the board later was enlarged to include businessmen Francisco Luna, John de la Garza, Jr., Reuben D. Martinez and Eugene Vilfordi.

A deal was struck to demolish the old parochial school building and build a new parish center in the area where the high rise was to be and behind the cathedral where the school had been located on Flora Street. Beneath the new building would be a multi-level underground garage serving both the Cathedral and the Meyerson Center. Ground was broken in 1995 and the project was completed in 1997. Enhancement of the Cathedral continued with the laying of a new tile roof that same year.

On June 14, 1998, the celebration of the centennial began with a ceremony marking the 100th anniversary of the laying of the cornerstone by Bishop Edward Joseph Dunne in 1898. Assessment of the overall condition of the Cathedral interior and exterior began in preparation for a major renovation.

*Reflected in the window of a nearby high rise office tower is the new bell tower, a different and important addition to the downtown skyline. Inset is water color painting of the Cathedral before the towers were added.*

A new rector was appointed July 1, 1999. For the first time a native son, Father Ramón Alvarez, who grew up in the parish, was named rector of the Cathedral. In 2000 a steering committee for the capital campaign of local business and arts leaders was established headed by Honorary Chairman James M. Moroney, Jr., and Chairman Neil O'Brien. The committee had an original goal of $20,000,000.

*Very Rev. Eduardo Gonzales rector of the Cathedral, named in 2006.*

*Architects rendering of the front of the Cathedral before and after the addition of the towers.*

Architexas, a firm of preservation and restoration architects was hired to guide the process and Andres Construction Services was chosen to manage and execute restoration, preservation and renovation projects. The master plan envisioned four phases, not necessarily in chronological order: the exterior restoration; the interior restoration; new construction; and key enhancements, which include the construction of a world-class pipe organ and a permanent endowment for preservation and maintenance.

Phase I included the construction of the bell towers and steeples; installation of the carillon, restoration of the stained glass windows and stonework, repair of the brick masonry, roof cresting and replacement of gutters and downspouts. Phase II involved interior restoration including: construction of a new altar, ambo and liturgical furnishings; installation of a new image of the Virgin of Guadalupe, restoration of the sanctuary including restoration of the side altars, the restoration of the original pews, installation of a new lighting system, expansion of the narthex, construction of a new sacristy, construction of a Chapel of Reservation, construction of a Chapel of Reconciliation and the restoration of the ceiling stencils and the wood beams.

*Pope John Paul II blesses the computer imaged copy of the tilma of St. Juan Diego in 2001 before its installation in the Cathedral sanctuary. Holding the image is Cathedral rector Father Alvarez, as Father Eduardo Gonzales, then pastor of St. Edward Church looks on.*

As work on the sanctuary renovation continued, the giant tapestry of Our Lady of Guadalupe was replaced with a smaller computer generated image of the actual tilma of St. Juan Diego. The new image was taken to Rome by Father Alvarez and a delegation from the Cathedral to be blessed by Pope John Paul II. When it was installed a two-foot gold crown was mounted above the new image. The tapestry was moved to the Great Hall in the parish center.

Repainting of the interior and blessing of a new marble altar in 2002 continued the restoration of the grandeur of the Cathedral. The refurbished

*Then Coadjutor Bishop Joseph Galante blesses the new Cathedral altar after its installation in 2002.*

pews and new flooring were in place for the visit of the relic of the original tilma of St. Juan Diego on September 14, 2003.

Celebration of the centennial continued with the publication of *Circuit Rider to Cathedral* a new history of the Diocese published for the occasion. On October 26, 2002, the 100th anniversary of the Cathedral was marked with a festive Liturgy and celebration.

*"Circuit Rider to Cathedral: How the Diocese of Dallas Came to Be" written by Diocesan Archivist Steve Landregan, was published to mark the Centenary of the Cathedral dedication in October 2002.*

*Renovation included the installation of a marble Gothic arch at the rear of the sanctuary to frame the new image of Our Lady of Guadalupe.*

Of special interest is the crown which is above the image of the Virgin of Guadalupe in the sanctuary of the Cathedral. It is similar to the crown over the original tilma of St. Juan Diego in the Basilica in Mexico City. The crown includes precious jewels donated by parishioners of the Cathedral.

Bishop Charles V. Grahmann placed the crown above the image of the Virgin in December of 2001. The image itself, a computer generated replica of the original, was blessed by Pope John Paul II on December 3, 2002, the 470th anniversary of the first apparition of Our Lady of Guadalupe to St. Juan Diego.

A special niche was created for the crown and it is protected by an alarm.

*The Crown that surmounts the image of the Virgin is inscribed with the words "Empress of the Americas," a title given Our Lady of Guadalupe in 1945 by Pope Pius XII.*

*Former Cathedral rector, Father Ramón Alvarez, celebrates Mass with the image of Our Lady of Guadalupe and the Crown shown in the background.*

# Culmination

*A crane hoists the largest of the carillon bells to the bell tower during final phases of construction.*

After more than 100 years the dream of Bishop Dunne and architect Nicholas Clayton began to be translated into reality with the contribution of $500,000 for a new carillon by Lynn and James Moroney, Jr., a descent of one of the original families.

The four and one half million dollars required for the construction of the two steeples and bell tower was raised thanks to the Moroney gift, other generous contributions and the determination of Bishop Grahmann. Ground was broken for the new bell tower on June 28, 2004 and it was dedicated with a carillon concert on September 11, 2005 performed by Gert Oldenbeuving, guest carillionneur from the Netherlands.

*Bishop Charles Grahmann blesses the carillon bells before their installation in the bell tower.*

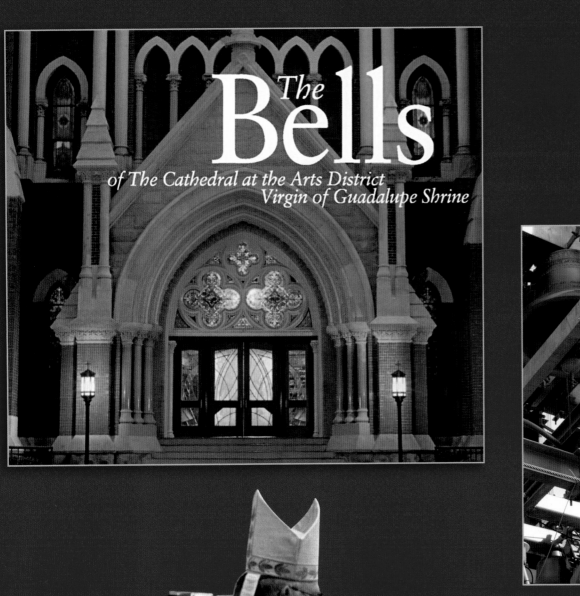

# The Bells

of The Cathedral at the Arts District
Virgin of Guadalupe Shrine

In his homily at the bell tower dedication Bishop Grahmann summed up the significance of the moment: "The architecture of any age in history reveals the deepest yearnings of the architect who attempts to capture the imagination of the people of a particular age. This Cathedral is no exception. To capture the heart of man's yearning for meaning and search for God, the beautiful tower and bells were a visible symbol. Reaching high into the skies, reaching for the divine, as if to touch and make contact with the author of all life, the tower interpreted this reality. Today we celebrate the culmination of that which realizes this desire."

Further enhancement of the Cathedral grounds was assured by a gift from the Catholic Foundation of a plaza on the corner of Flora and Crockett streets opposite the Meyerson Center.

Much of the Phase I renovation has been accomplished and restoration continues on both the interior and the exterior. Phase III involves new construction and remains to be addressed, including a Cathedral auditorium and salon on the northeast corner of the property and Guadalupe Plaza on the southeast corner of the campus. Phase IV includes the construction and installation of a concert pipe organ, audio and video production facilities and, most importantly the establishment of a Preservation and Maintenance Endowment to ensure that the community's

*In 2005, the 50th anniversary of the Catholic Foundation, the construction of a plaza on the corner of Crocket and Flora was funded by the Foundation.*

investment in the Cathedral is protected and is preserved for future generations.

Through the efforts of the Cathedral Restoration and Preservation Fund, Inc., the Cathedral has become more than the seat of the Catholic Diocese. It is a significant community asset with generous support from all segments of the Dallas community.

With the collaboration of the Arts District neighbors and the civic and business communities, the First Cathedral Gala was held in November 2005. The participants celebrated the progress of

renovation, completion of the steeples, bell tower, carillon and the new sanctuary.

There is substantial community support for the Cathedral. The complete success of the Gala (a fundraiser) demonstrated this. The Cathedral in the Dallas Arts District is recognized as an important cultural and religious shrine by Catholics and all others.

*A blessing for the Matachina dancers is given by Bishop Grahmann following the celebration of the feast day of Our Lady of Guadalupe. Attending the bishop are Deacons Alberto Villarreal, left, and Charles Stump.*

# Nicholas Clayton

Nicholas Clayton was the first registered architect in Texas. Like so many of his contemporaries he immigrated to the United States as a child, when his widowed mother brought him from County Cork, Ireland to Cincinnati in 1840 when he was seven years old.

He served as a plasterer, stone carver and draftsman in his youth, and served in the Union Navy during the Civil War. In 1871 he moved to Houston, but within a few months he moved to Galveston, which at the time was Texas' largest city. By 1880 he had become the leading architect in the city.

Many of his buildings designed at that time remain today. Along the Strand, Galveston's primary commercial street, may be found many of the commercial buildings he designed for the city's bankers and merchants. In the East End residential neighborhood many of his grand homes still stand.

It was during the 1880s, when Dallas for the first and only time became Texas' largest city, that Clayton designed the first portion of Ursuline Academy in what was then East Dallas. The first phase was completed in 1882 but he continued to add to the facility until 1907.

It was likely that it was during Clayton's first work on Ursuline that Father Joseph Martiniere, then pastor of Sacred Heart Church, came in contact with him. Clayton's records in the Rosenberg Museum in Galveston indicate that he was first contacted in 1887 about building a "cathedral" in Dallas. It would be three years before Dallas would become a diocese so one can only speculate about Martiniere's 1887 "cathedral."

Clayton's original design went through many modifications, mostly budgetary downsizing before a final commission came from Bishop Edward Joseph Dunne to begin construction in 1898, but without the spires designed by the architect. Sacred Heart Cathedral was completed in 1902 and dedicated on October 26 of that year.

Over time, the credit for the cathedral design became associated with Bishop Dunne and not Clayton, but records found in recent years and turned over to the Rosenberg library have established with certainty that Clayton was the cathedral's architect.

Those same records fail to show that Nicholas Clayton was ever paid for his work.

Neither Bishop Dunne nor Clayton lived to see the completion of his cathedral, but his grandson, Michael J. Clayton, was present for the occasion in September 2005.

# Celebration

*Consecration of the Sacred Chrism includes the Bishop breathing on the chrism after adding the Oil of Balsam. Sacred Chrism is used in Ordinations, Confirmation and certain other blessings*

*Containers of oils are brought to the altar at the Mass of the Chrism, the first celebration of Holy Week. One container will be consacreted as Holy Chrism by the bishop, the other two will be blessed as the Oil of the Sick and the Oil of Catechumens. Carrying the oils are Deacons Rick Harrington, left, and Brian Mitchell.*

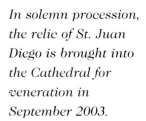

*In solemn procession, the relic of St. Juan Diego is brought into the Cathedral for veneration in September 2003.*

*Central to the office of Bishop is the ordination of men to the priesthood and the diaconate. The laying on hands by the Bishop is the ancient symbol of passing on the power of office dating back to the Old Testament where Moses laid hands on his successor, Joshua.*

67

The Book of Gospels leads the entrance procession whenever an Eucharist Liturgy is included. The prominence given the Book of Gospels reflects the presence of God in the Word.

Many processions, like this one marking Pro-Life Sunday, wend their way to the Cathedral for celebrations.

The ram's horn has been used to call believers to worship since Old Testament times.

*Incense used in liturgical rituals symbolize prayers of the faithful rising to God. Ceremonial incensing often precedes special celebrations.*

*The Easter Vigil Service begins with the blessing of the new fire, from which the Easter Candle is lighted and carried into the darkened Cathedral, symbolizing the arrival of the Light of Christ.*

69

*Thousands crowed into the Cathedral to mourn the death and celebrate the life of Pope John Paul II in April 2005.*

*A bell choir adds a festive note at special celebrations.*

At pontifical celebrations, the Bishop presides from the Cathedra, representing the seat of his Episcopal power. The Cathedral is so called because it is the site of the Cathedral.

As the welcoming center of the Diocese, the Cathedral draws many diverse worshippers, lay and religious, such as these Missionaries of Charity of Mother Teresa's community.

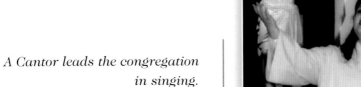

A Cantor leads the congregation in singing.

A new bride follows the ancient tradition of placing flowers before the image of the Blessed Virgin.

The Catholic Foundation celebrated fifty years of service to the Diocese of Dallas in 2005 with a Eucharistic Liturgy and reception. The Foundation also made a gift of a new plaza at Flora and Crockett Streets to mark their golden jubilee.

# Stained glass and statues

*A crowned statue of Our Lady of Guadalupe is a feature of the prayer chapel located in the original Baptistery.*

Stained glass and statues were the first catechisms. Christians learned of the lives of the saints and the stories of creation and salvation through the magic of art. The beautiful stained glass windows in the Cathedral are a visual history of our diocese, memorializing and commemorating the men and women who founded and maintained our community for more than a century, and the communities that comprised this portion of God's vineyard.

*For over a century this statue has stood in blessing before the Cathedral congregations. It is presently located on the side altar to the West of the sanctuary.*

*A Pieta, depicting Mary with the body of Jesus, is located on the East side at the rear of the Cathedral.*

*Our Lady of Cobra, patroness of Cuba, was a gift of the Cuban community that came to Dallas following the Communist revolution. Many refugee groups have first been welcomed to Dallas at the Cathedral.*

The Yom Hashoah
Menorah
was presented to
Bishop Grahmann
by the Center for
Interreligious
Understanding.
The Menorah is
a replica of one
presented to
Pope John Paul II
in 1999.

*A statue of
the Sacred Heart,
patron of the Diocese
of Dallas, stands high
above the front entrance
to the Cathedral.*

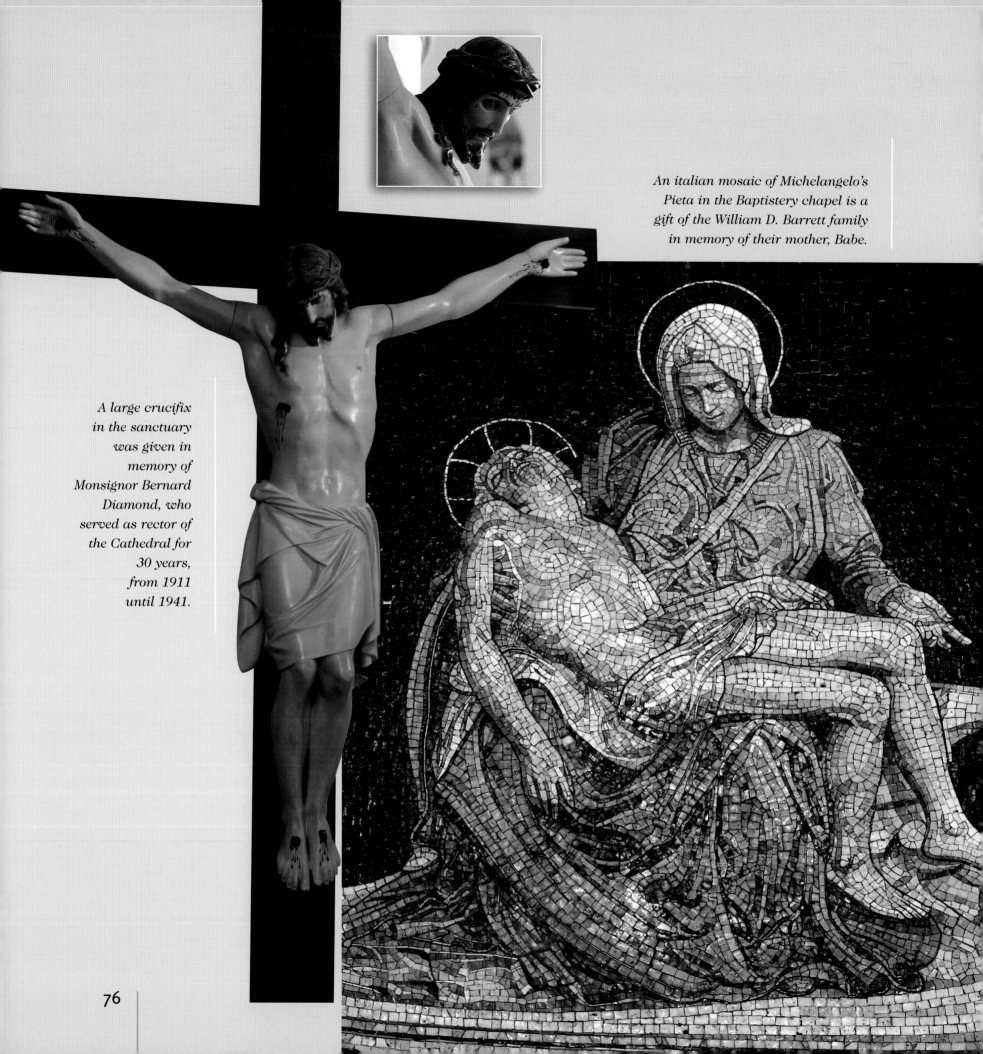

An italian mosaic of Michelangelo's
Pieta in the Baptistery chapel is a
gift of the William D. Barrett family
in memory of their mother, Babe.

A large crucifix
in the sanctuary
was given in
memory of
Monsignor Bernard
Diamond, who
served as rector of
the Cathedral for
30 years,
from 1911
until 1941.

*The adoring angel statues on the side altar of Eucharistic*
*Reservation, were the gifts of Esperanza and Juanita Nañez*
*in memory of their parents, Eulalio and Aurelia Nañez.*

*St. James the Major*

*Nun*
*Donated by*
*Gainesville*

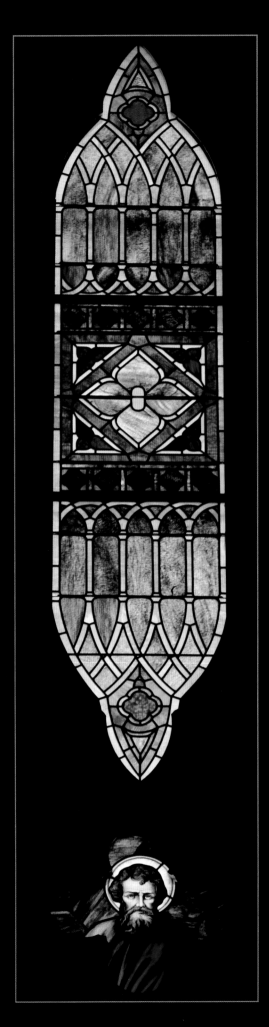

*Clerestory
Windows*

# Cities of the diocese

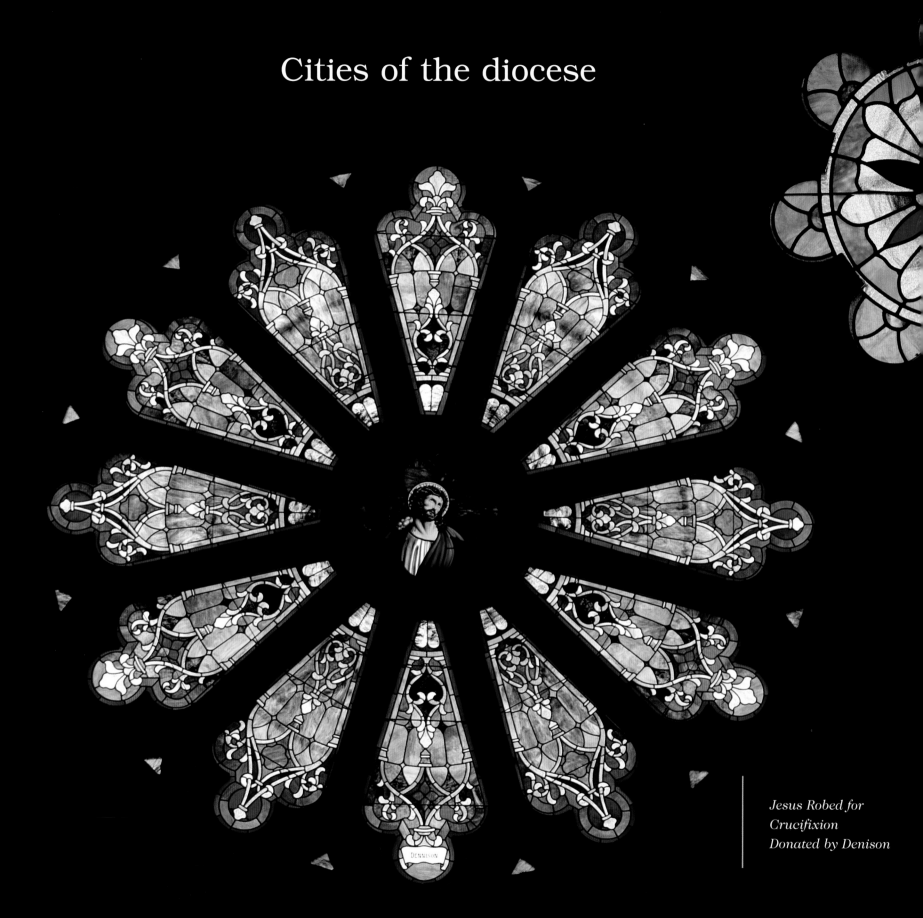

*Jesus Robed for*
*Crucifixion*
*Donated by Denison*

*Mater Dolorosa*
*Donated by Sherman*

Clerestory Windows donated by parishes and individuals in 1902.

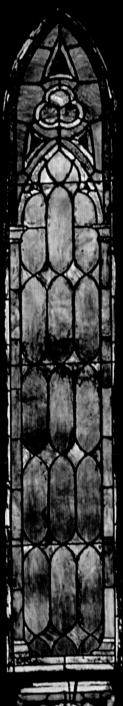

*Clarksville*          *Hillsboro*          *Waxahachie*          *Mrs. C. Laudermilk*          *MicKinney*

Thurber

Lindsey

Unnamed

Bonham

Clarendon

# Symbol windows

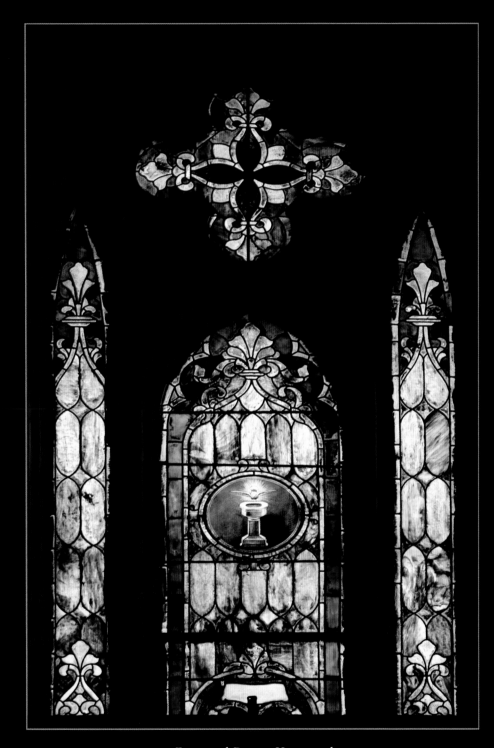

Font and Dove - Unnamed

Crown & Cross – Windhorst

*Jesus in a Crown of Thorns - Terrell*

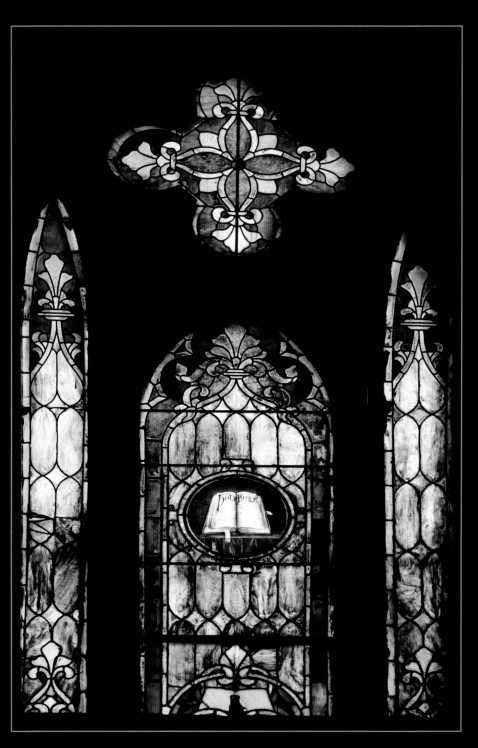

*Holy Bible - Unnamed*

# Symbol windows

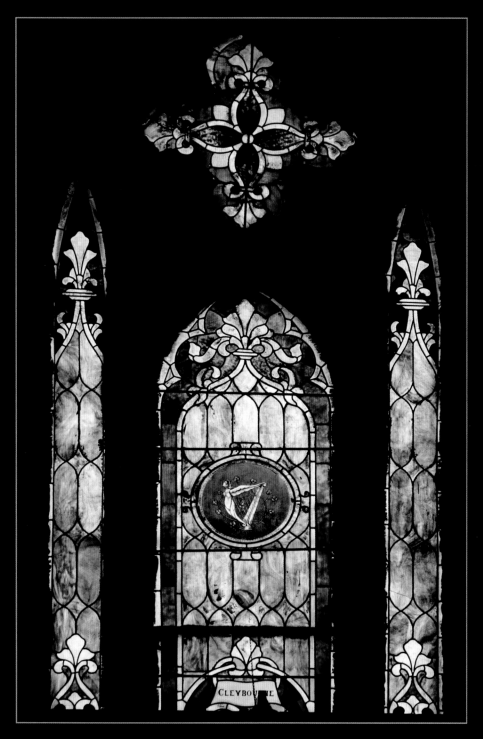

*Harp/Lyre with Female Figure – Cleburne*

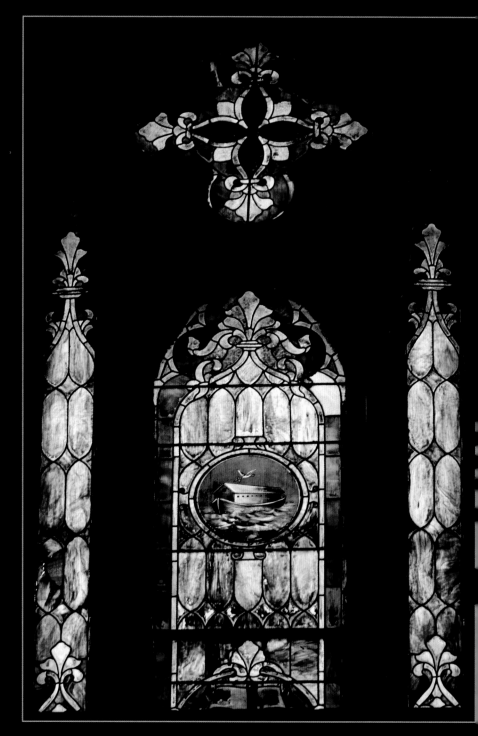

*Noah's Ark – Unnamed*

*Papal Keys – Ennis*

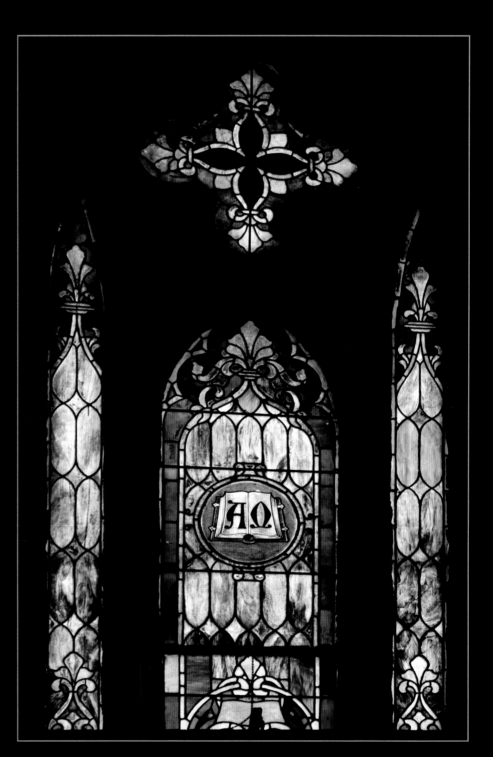

*Alpha and Omega Book – Unnamed*

# Symbol windows

*Deus, Pater, Filius, Spiritus – St. Paul*

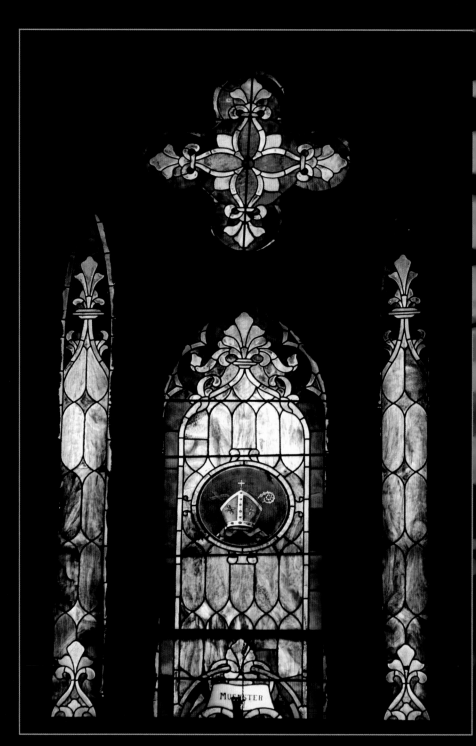

*Bishop's Miter, Crozier and Cross – Muenster*

*Papal Tiara and Papal Keys – Unnamed*

*Ten Commandments Tablet – Unnamed*

# Nuns' windows

*From the Sisters
of the Incarnate Word*

*From The Ursuline Nuns*

*From Sisters
of St. Mary of Namur*

# Miscellaneous memorial windows

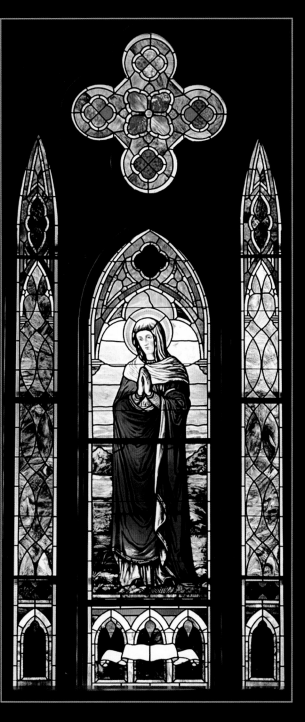

*St. Ann*
*Restored in Honor of Our Parents*
*Isabel and Lawrence Ackels*
*The Ackels Family*

*St. John the Evangelist*
*Donated in 1902*
*In Memory of the Deceased*
*Members of the Fleming Family*

*Bishop*
*Donated in 1902*
*Reverend Joseph Granger*

# Memorial Windows

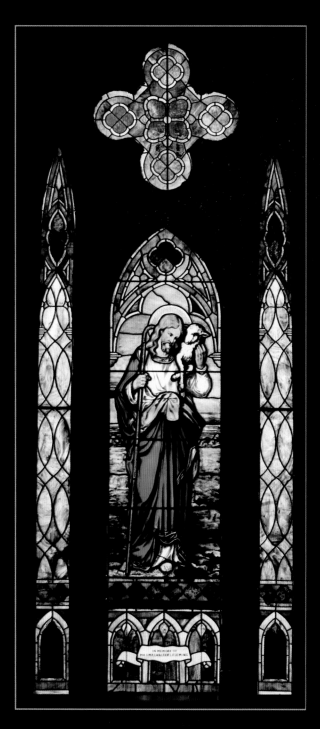

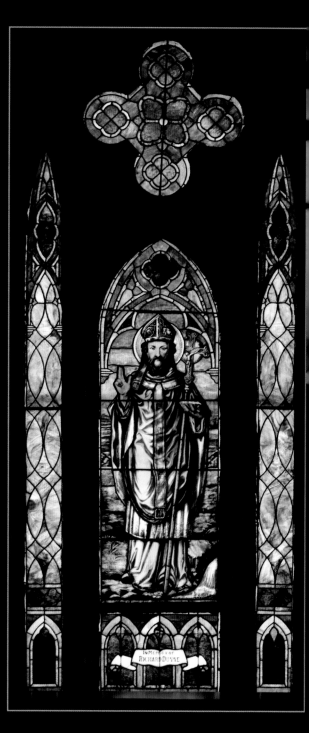

*Jesus the Good Shepherd donated in 1902*
*in Memory of Mr. & Mrs. Walter L. Fleming*
*Restored in Honor*
*of Helen and John W. Mullen, Jr.*

*Bishop with heart*
*Donated in 1902*
*Edward A. Bergin*

*Bishop with Cross*
*Donated in 1902*
*In Memory of Richard Dunne*

*St. Peter*
*Donated in 1902 by*
*Daniel And Mary Cullen*
*Restored by*
*Monsignor Leon Duesman*
*In Honor of*
*The Most Reverend Thomas A.*
*Tschoepe*

*St. Matthew*
*Donated in 1902 by*
*T.F. O'Cara*

*St. Bartholomew*
*Donated in 1902 by*
*Dennis Hayes*
*Restored in Honor of*
*The Vogel and O'Brien Families*

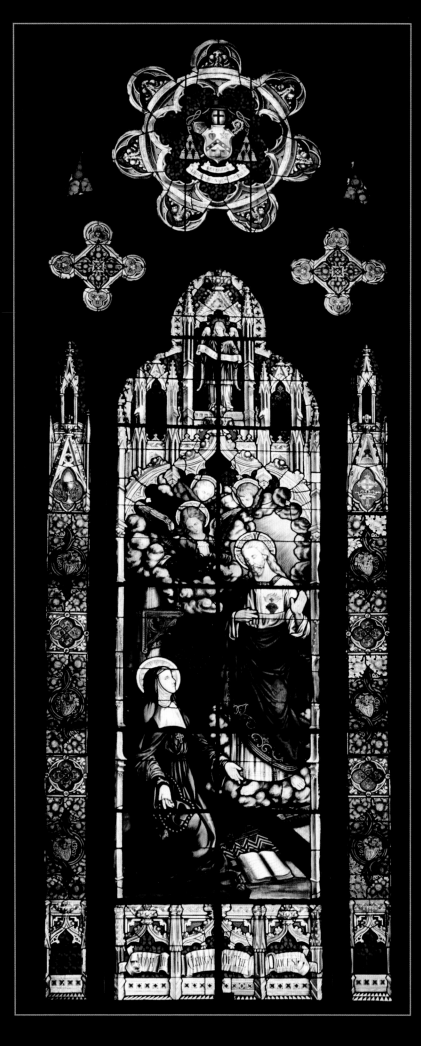

# Main
# window
# above
# altar

*Donated in 1902*
*by the Clergy of*
*Diocese Dallas*

*Windows in the tower were restored through gifts from
Mary Ellen and Dave Fox, Shirley and Gene Vilfordi*

# Construction

Months of planning went into the design and construction of the bell tower and steeples and the equipment required for the carillon. When architect Nicholas Clayton and Bishop Dunne envisioned the towers over a century ago they could never have envisioned the technology that enabled architects today to translate their dreams into reality.

It was necessary to construct a new steel frame inside the existing short towers to support the new towers and the bells. From hidden excavations deep beneath the existing cathedral to workmen hoisted high above the cathedral to remove the protective cover from the gold leaf cross that topped the new steeple, the genius of architects and the labor of countless skilled construction workers were required to bring the project to completion.

*A great steel skeleton had to fabricated to fit inside the origin Cathedral tower to carry the additional weigh of the carillon and steeple. This picture shows the top of the steel skeleton just after it had been hoisted by a crane and dropped into the tower.*

*Final assembly of the clavier had to be done after it was hoisted to its permanent position near the top of the tower.*

*High in the bell tower is the carillon keyboard that creates the melodies that waft over downtown Dallas.*

*Final brickwork is added after the carillon bells and new steeple and cross have been hoisted to the top and bolted in place (opposite page).*

*Workmen
are dwarfed
by the size of
the large carillon
bells as they
assemble and
manhandle them
prior to hoisting
them to the tower.*

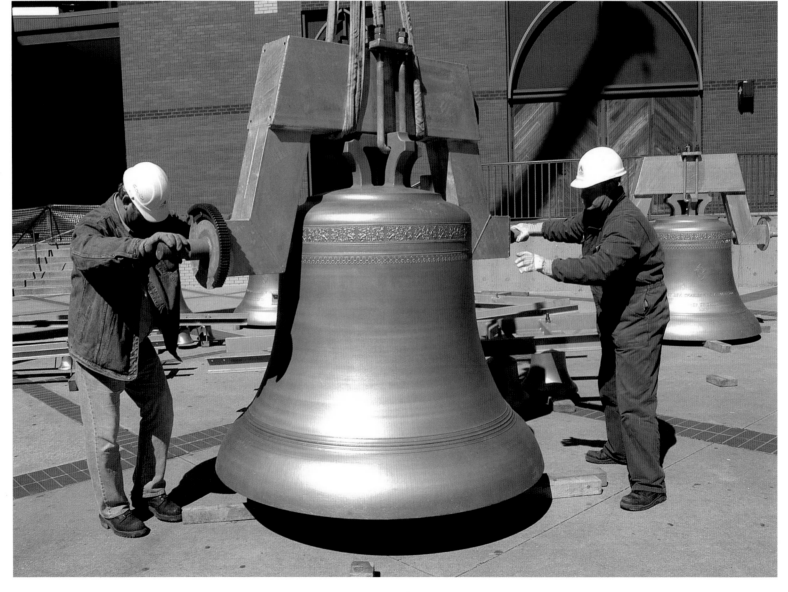

*Bells of the carillon finally are in place
in the bell tower after months of planning.
Only the brickwork remains.*

# Renovation

It is more correct to speak of restoration and renovation because the continuing program of the Cathedral is both to restore the building and many of its furnishings to their original condition and to replace and renovate where restoration is not possible or practical or changing liturgical requirements necessitate a change.

The Master Plan for renovation developed in 1999 determined that the Cathedral renovation/restoration should be in four phases, not necessarily in chronological order. The phases would embrace exterior restoration, interior restoration and new construction, construction of a world-class pipe organ and the establishment of a permanent endowment for preservation and maintenance.

*Prominent in the renovated sanctuary is the Cathedra or Bishop's Chair.*

G RELIGION

The Dallas Morning News

*Spirituality & Values*

INSIDE

**Travels with the pope**

Staff Writer Frank Trejo recalls two papal tours. 4G

DallasNews.com Saturday, February 26, 200

# *Inspired* vision

## Dallas cathedral's bell tower will complete architect's dream

By COLLEEN McCAIN NELSON
Staff Writer

The tall, graceful tower to the left doesn't exist — not yet.

But it will, very soon.

The downtown Catholic cathedral is staking out a spot in the Dallas skyline. Brick by brick, a 20-story bell tower is rising above the Arts District. With 49 brass bells, it will bring music to the corner of Ross Avenue and Pearl Street.

The project, part of a multimillion-dollar restoration, has been more than a century in the making. **More, 6G**

**RINGING IN THE NEW** *Following noon Mass on Tuesday, the bells for the new tower will be blessed in a ceremony on the cathedral plaza. Dallas Bishop Charles Grahmann is scheduled to preside.*

Graphics by LAYNE SMITH, SERGIO PEÇANHA and DEAN HOLLINGSWORTH

### REACHING UP TO THE SKY

The $4.9 million main tower rises to 224 feet. Besides adorning the cathedral, its main function is to hold a carillon, a musical instrument composed of a keyboard, called a clavier, and 49 pure bronze bells.


400 feet
Woodall Rodgers
Flora
Pearl
Ross
Dallas Catholic Cathedral
New tower
Second new steeple


**CROSS**
Made of aluminium tubing with gold leaf finish, it is just over 11 feet tall.

### THE MUSICAL INSTRUMENT

The bells are made of bronze and have a range of four octaves. The bells are precisely tuned to ensure accurate tones.


Largest bell
Smallest bell
5ft 10in
5ft 10in (7,500 lbs)
8 in (22 lbs)


**BELL CHAMBER**
Only the four biggest bells swing. Operated by gearwheel transmission, they don't require chains like older models.


Headstocks of galvanized steel
Gearwheel transmission
The 45 smaller bells are static, operated by hammers
Front view
Side view
Front view
Clavier
Wires connect the clavier to the bells
Keyboard
Pedals


**CARILLONNEUR'S OFFICE**
This is where the musician (carillonneur) plays the bells using the clavier, an instrument similar to an organ with large keys. The bells can also be played by computer.

### SUPPORT FOR THE TOWER

The load-bearing walls and foundation of the original tower would not have been adequate to support the enormous weight of the bells. A steel frame was lowered into the tower's existing facade to carry the weight.


Steel frame
Existing structure
Ground level
Foundation
Piers


**THE STEEPLE**
Two steeples made of copper and adorned with a diamond-like pattern will cap the church's tall and shorter towers.

**PRACTICE CLAVIER**
A second clavier will be installed in the east tower. This one will not be directly connected to bells but will allow the musician to practice. A computer can record notes for playback by the bells in the main tower.

### THE FOUNDATION

Engineers cut through parts of the existing foundation and threaded over 200 pounds of rebar in several layers. Then they added concrete beneath and within the existing foundation, providing support for the massive steel skeleton. Piers were driven 54 feet deep and into bedrock to provide additional support.


Pier
4 feet of concrete and rebar
Existing brick foundation


SOURCES: Cathedral; ARCHITEXAS; Andres Construction; *Dallas Morning News* research.

### ABOUT THE ARCHITECT

Nicholas J. Clayton was born in Cork, Ireland, around 1839 and emigrated in 1851. After learning architecture in Memphis, Tenn., he moved to Galveston in 1872. In addition to the cathedral, his works include Gresham House (1888) and the University of Texas Medical School Building (1889-90), both in Galveston.

*On February 26, 2005, the Dallas Morning News published a full page article and artwork by Layne Smith, Sergio Peçanha and Dean Hollingsworth which outlined the construction of the bell tower and installation of the carillon. (Courtesy of the Dallas Morning News)*

Phase I has been partially completed. It included the construction of the bell towers and steeples; installation of the carillon, restoration of the stained glass windows and stonework, repair of the brick masonry, roof cresting and replacement of gutters and downspouts. The bell towers and steeples have been completed, the carillon is installed, work has begun on the stained-glass window restoration but much work remains on the exterior stonework and brick masonry. Nothing has been done on the roof cresting and downspouts.

Phase II has begun but is far from completed. A new altar has been installed and consecrated, a new ambo has been installed and a new image of the Virgin of Guadalupe has been installed and crowned. Some liturgical furnishings have been restored or replaced. The original pews have been removed and restored. Still remaining is the installation of a new lighting system, expansion of the narthex, construction of a new sacristy, construction of a Chapel of Reservation, construction of a Chapel of Reconciliation and the restoration of the ceiling stencils and the wood beams.

Phase III remains to be addressed. It involves new construction including a Cathedral auditorium and salon on the northeast corner of the property and Guadalupe Plaza on the southeast corner of the campus.

Phase IV includes the construction and installation of a concert pipe organ, audio and video production facilities and, most importantly the establishment of a Preservation and Maintenance Endowment to ensure that the community's investment in the Cathedral is protected and is preserved for future generations.

Shakespeare once wrote "What is past is prologue", past accomplishments set the agenda for the future. Much has been accomplished in the restoration and renovation of the cathedral, but much must be done. In truth, maintenance of this community treasure is a continuing challenge not only to Catholics but to the entire community of Dallas and to the arts district for which it provides a spiritual anchor and link to our history.

Proceeds from the annual Cathedral Gala and the continued generosity of Dallas citizens will provide the endowment to insure that our treasure is passed on to future generations.

*Among the many restoration projects remaining is the replacement of deteriorating stone on much of the cathedral exterior.*

*The carilloneur can save a climb to the top of the bell tower for rehearsals by using this practice carillon located in the shorter East tower. The instrument may also be used to record programs to be played on the tower carillon.*

*Renovations of the Cathedral sacristy include refinishing of the massive oak cabinet/wardrobe where vestments, linens and ecclesiastical appointments are stored.*

*Long-range renovation plans include a new state of the art pipe organ. This historic organ will be preserved and housed in another location at the Cathedral.*

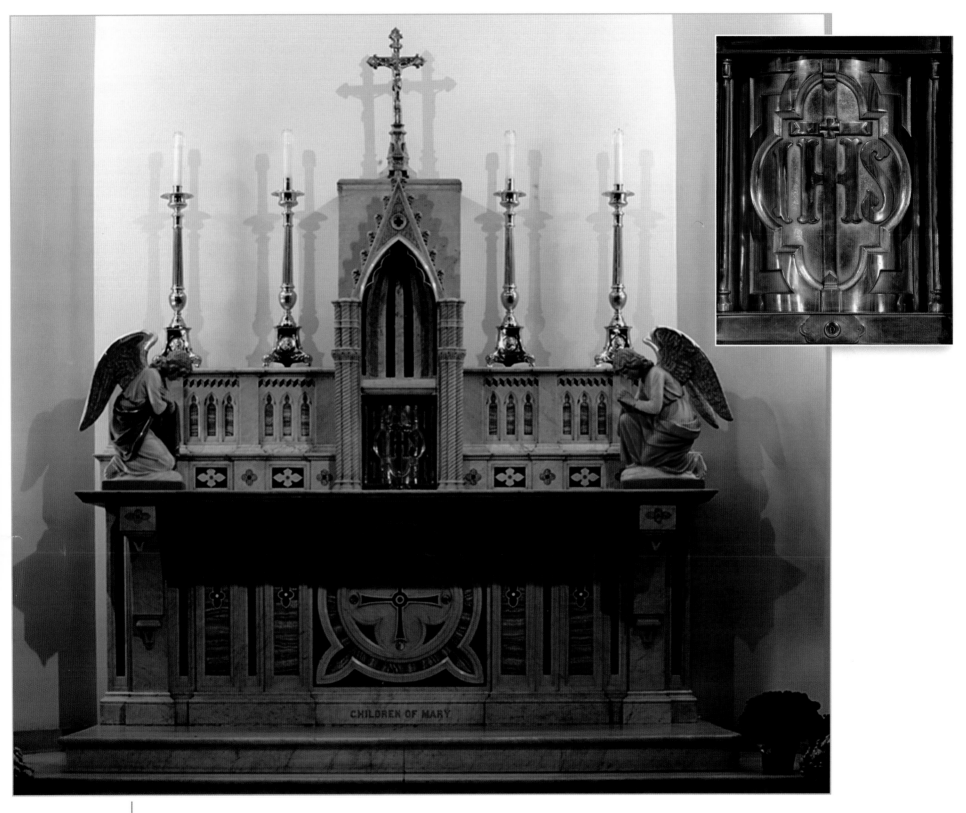

*Formerly one of four side altars, this altar on the East of the sanctuary now serves as the altar of Eucharistic reservation.*

# Stations of the Cross

Great care was taken in the renovation of the fourteen original Stations of the Cross that have been returned to their original beauty.

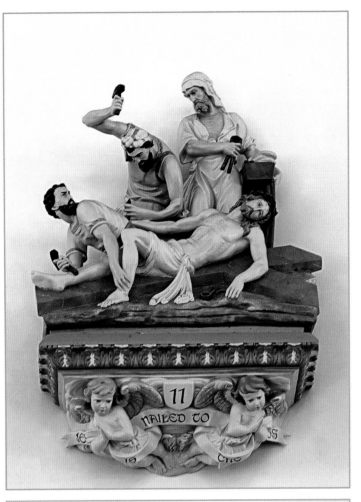

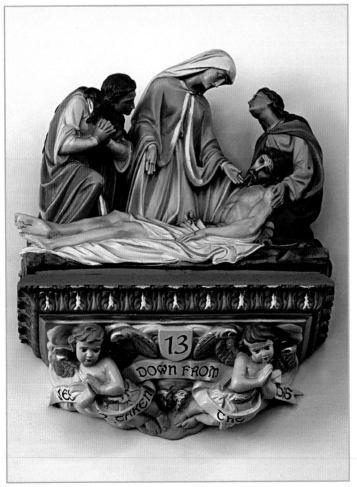

The Gala Committee *and* Advisory Council
Raymond D. Nasher, Honorary Chairman,

cordially invite you *to*
The First Annual Cathedral *at the* Arts District Gala

Thursday, November 17, *at* 6:30 p.m.
2215 Ross Avenue

Concert *in the* Cathedral *by*
Daniel Rodriguez, 9-11 Singing Police Officer, *and*
Suzanna Guzmán, Mezzo Soprano, Los Angeles Opera

Candlelight dinner *to follow in*
The Morton H. Meyerson Symphony Center

Valet parking *on* Crockett Street

R.S.V.P.                                                    Black Tie

Benefitting the Cathedral Restoration & Preservation Fund, Inc.

*Daniel Rodriguez*
*welcomes guests*
*to the Cathedral*
*Concert with his*
*opening song.*

*Honorary Chairman
Raymond D. Nasher is
joined in the left by Charles
and Cindy Gummer
and on the right by Linda
and John DiFede.*

*The Ed Bernet Trio
entertained during
the candlelight dinner.*

Lydia and Dan Novakov
were among the guests
who enjoyed the candlelight
dinner at the Meyerson following
the Cathedral Concert.

Gene and Shirley Vilfordi enjoyed the visiting
and music at the Meyerson dinner.

At one of the many
planning sessions for
the Gala were, from left,
Co-Chairs Stewart
and Christy Frazer,
Underwriting Party Hosts
John and Carole Lee and
Co-Chairs Dona and
Reuben Martinez.

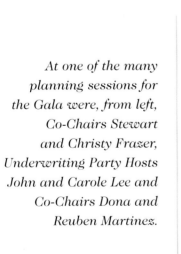

*Executive Chef Tim Semunuk
and Co-Chairs Reuben and Dona Martinez
take a break during the busy evening.*

*Singing Policeman
Daniel Rodriguez relaxes
with Virginia Monday
after his performance.*

*Episcopal Vicar
Monsignor Milam Joseph,
Tom Unis, Jr., and
David Saller were
probably talking
about Notre Dame's next
game at the dinner.*

# Chronology

- 1846:

Dallas County created out of Nacogdoches County to the East and Robertson County to the West, the Village of Dallas is designated temporary County Seat.

- 1850:

Dallas beats out Cedar Springs and Hord's Ridge in a three-way race for permanent County Seat.

- 1852:

Maxime Guillot, the first known Catholic citizen, moves to Dallas from Fort Worth and sets up a business manufacturing carriages and wagons.

- 1854:

Father Michael Sheehan, a priest of the Diocese of Galveston, is appointed a full time chaplain at Fort Belknap in Young County. He serves there until 1859 and occasionally visits the Catholics in Dallas.

- 1855:

Victor Considerant establishes La Réunion Colony, a commune of French speaking atheistic-social-democrats, on the West side of the Trinity. Maxime Guillot acts as interpreter for the colonists and as general liaison with the commune.

Bishop Jean Marie Odin of Galveston sends his Vicar General, Father Louis Chambodut to visit the La Réunion Colony and nearby communities including Dallas.

- 1856:

In a letter to the Propagation of the Faith in Rome, Bishop Odin reports on Father Chambodut's two month journey to North Texas and reports, among other things, that he found seven "anglo-Catholic" families in Dallas eager for a priest.

- 1857:

Bishop Odin sends Father Claude Dubuis to visit La Réunion a second time.

● 1858:

La Réunion Colony fails. Many of the colonists return to France but others remain purchasing land from the failed commune and setting up businesses in Dallas and other area villages.

● 1859:

Father Sebastian Auguneur, a missionary from Nacogdoches, celebrates the first recorded Mass in Dallas in the home of Maxime Guillot. The Guillot family and two single men, identified only as Carey and Walsh, are present.

● 1868:

A mission station and residence are established at St. Paul in Collin County where a group of Irish immigrants settled and built a church. Father Joseph Martiniere and Father Thomas Hennesy minister to Catholics in Dallas from St. Paul.

● 1872:

Bishop Claude Dubuis of Galveston establishes a parish in Dallas and sends Father Mathurin Perrier as first pastor. Parish meets for one year at Odd Fellows Hall and vote to name the parish Sacred Heart of Jesus.

The first railroad, the Houston and Texas Central, reaches Dallas.

● 1873:

Father Perrier purchases a lot on the corner of Bryan and Masten streets for $500 and begins construction of a frame church. The church is completed in about three months and the first Mass is celebrated the first Sunday of August in 1873.

The second railroad, the Texas and Pacific, reaches Dallas from the East and temporarily ceases construction due to the financial panic of 1873 making Dallas the railhead during the great buffalo drives. Dallas becomes world buffalo hide market.

December, Father Joseph Martiniere is named pastor of Sacred Heart Church to succeed Father Perrier.

● 1874:

Father Martiniere purchases adjoining lot for future school. In one year the price went from $500 to $3,700. A small frame building is built on the lot to serve as a school.

Six Ursuline nuns agree to come to Dallas from

the Galveston Community to establish a school. Sacred Heart parochial school opens February 2 with seven pupils.

● 1875:

A larger two-story frame school building is built. Ursulines take over teaching of a boys school that will later become St. Patrick's Parochial School.

● 1882:

Bishop of Galveston establishes a second Dallas Parish, St. Patrick. Church built on Cabell St. on land donated by Houston and Texas Central Railroad.

Construction begins on Ursuline Academy designed by Nicholas Clayton on property purchased on East Side of Dallas.

● 1884:

Ursuline Academy opens. Sisters move to new convent and school but continue teaching at Sacred Heart Parochial School.

● 1888:

Father Martiniere contacts architect Nicholas Clayton about drawing up plans for a "Dallas Cathedral."

● 1889:

Father Martiniere resigns as pastor of Sacred Heart to serve as chaplain for Ursuline Academy and Ursuline nuns.

Father Joseph Blum becomes third pastor of Sacred Heart Church. He purchases a new parish site on Ross Avenue for $30,000 with permission of Bishop Gallagher.

● 1890:

Pope Leo XIII establishes the Diocese of Dallas covering 108,000 square miles of North Texas extending from Louisiana to New Mexico.

Monsignor Thomas Francis Brennan of Erie, Pennsylvania, is named first Bishop of Dallas.

● 1891:

Bishop Brennan arrives in Dallas April 26 on the Houston and Texas Central. Because no cathedral church was designated in Pope Leo XII's bull of establishment, Bishop Brennan designates Sacred Heart Church as Pro-Cathedral. He announces his intention of building a new cathedral as soon as possible.

● 1892:

Bishop Brennan resigns. Financial problems prevented the construction of a cathedral.

● 1893:

Father Edward Joseph Dunne, pastor of All Saints Parish in Chicago, is named second Bishop of Dallas on September 24, 1893.

● 1894:

Bishop Dunne orders that planning should begin for the construction of a new cathedral on the Ross avenue site acquired by Father Blum. Dallas priests had presented Bishop Dunne with a $2,000 burse upon his arrival. Gifts from Chicago priests and friends to Bishop Dunne totaled $35,000 which he committed to the costs of the cathedral. He declines the offer of an Episcopal residence and chooses to live upstairs in the cathedral rectory.

● 1896:

After rejecting Nicholas Clayton's first and second proposals for the new cathedral as too expensive, Bishop Dunne orders a third and more modest proposal.

● 1897:

Father Blum becomes impatient with the lack of progress in building the cathedral and resigns as rector.

Father Jeoffrey A. Hartnett, the first priest ordained for the Diocese of Dallas, is appointed rector.

● 1898:

Ground is broken for the new cathedral after plans are altered to eliminate the two towers, proposed by Nicholas Clayton, for lack of funds.

● 1899:

Father Hartnett dies of smallpox during an epidemic in Dallas. He contracts the disease when called upon to minister to a dying woman at the pest house.

Father James Hayes is named rector.

● 1900:

Bishop Dunne intensifies his personal efforts to raise funds for the cathedral making many trips to the North and East to visit parishes and dioceses seeking help. Parishes in the diocese are asked to donate windows or other items. Local catholics are asked to memorialize friends and relatives with stained-glass windows.

● 1901:

Fund raising efforts by the Bishop result in many generous gifts from individuals and parishes within and outside the diocese. The Archbishop of Boston donates the organ, the priests of the Archdiocese of Chicago donate the great rose window. The priests of the Dallas diocese donate the windows above the altar. Many parishes and individuals memorialize windows.

● 1902:

On October 26, 1902, the Cathedral of the Sacred Heart is dedicated with great ceremony and celebration.

● 1904:

The old pro-cathedral is dismantled and rebuilt as St. Peter Claver Church to serve Black Catholics. An Episcopal residence is built for Bishop Dunne on West Davis Street in Oak Cliff.

● 1909:

Father J. S. O'Connor is named administrator.

● 1911:

Father Bernard H. Diamond is named rector
First Diocesan Synod held.

● 1914:

Storefront mission for Mexican refugees opened on Griffith Street by Fr. Manuel de Francisco, CM.

● 1918:

Griffith Street mission established as Our Lady of Guadalupe Parish.

● 1920:

Cathedral rectory is built.

● 1925:

Cathedral redecorated and beautified - new rectory.

● 1942:

Rev. Wilfred J. Bender named rector.

● 1948:

Rev. John T. Gulczynski named rector.

● 1952:

Rev. William F. O'Brien named rector.

● 1961:

Rev. Thomas Tschoepe named rector.

● 1965:

Sacred Heart Cathedral merged with Our Lady of Guadalupe Parish. Carmelite Fathers contracted to staff the Cathedral. Rev. Sebastian Valles, OCD named rector.

● 1966:

Rev. Denis Lynch, OCD, named as rector.

Cathedral Sanctuary Remodeled to conform to Vatican II.

● 1968:

Parochial School Closes.

● 1969:

Rev. Patrick Ahern, OCD, named as rector.

● 1972:

Rev. Andrew Palermo, OCD, named as rector.

● 1974:

Rev. Jenaro de la Cruz, OCD, named as rector.

● 1977:

Cathedral name officially changed by Vatican.

Tapestry of Our Lady of Guadalupe by Fr. B.G. Eades is blessed and installed in santuary.

● 1985:

Long-term lease with Bright Banc (Bright realty).

● 1986:

Cathedral Rectory demolished.

● 1986:

Sacred Heart School Demolished.

Contract with Carmelites rewritten.

● 1987:

Rev. Felix DaPrato, OCD, named as rector.

● 1988:

Rev. Lawrence Pichard, named as rector.

● 1990:

New tile roof on Cathedral.

● 1995:

Ground broken for parish center.

● 1998:

Centennial of Cornerstone laying – June 14.

● 1999:

Rev. Ramon Alvarez, named as rector.

● 2000:

Restoration/Renovation begun.

● 2001:

New Guadalupe Image – Blessed by Holy Father.

● 2001:

Save the Cathedral campaign.

● 2002:

Altar and shrine consecrated.

● 2003:

New Pews and Floor.

● 2003:

Visitation of the relic of the tilma of St. Juan Diego. (Sept. 14).

● 2004:

Ground broken for new bell tower on June 28.

● 2005:

Foundation gift for plaza

Dedication of Bell Tower Sept 11, 2005.

● 2006:

Rev. Eduardo Gonzáles named rector.

# Acknowledgements

**Cathedral Restoration & Preservation Fund, Inc.**
**Board of Directors**

Most Reverend Charles V. Grahmann, D.D.

Reverend Eduardo Gonzáles

Francisco Luna

Reuben D. Martinez

Eugene E. Vilfordi

Christy L. Frazer Ex-officio

Director of Development

**Capital Campaign Steering Committee**

James M. Moroney, Jr. Honorary Chairman

Neil J. O'Brien, Chairman

Jan Collmer

Harlan R. Crow

John A. Cuellar

Michael A. Gonzales

Reverend Gilbert J. Graham, O.P.

Edmond Haggar

M. Laurette Hesser

Richard M. Hull

William A. McCormack

Julio Medina

Raymond D. Nasher

Susan H. Stahl

Robert E. Sulentic

Kip Tindell

John Tolle

Eugene E. Vilfordi

Martin J. Weiland

**Cathedral Restoration & Preservation Fund**
**Committee**

Very Reverend Ramón Alvarez, V.F.

Reverend Monsignor Robert Coerver

Reverend Monsignor Michael Duca

Brian Bentley

Ruben Castro

Pedro Davila

John Debner

Christy L. Frazer

Felix Garza

Deacon Larry Harmon

Alice Hernandez

Laurette Hesser

Norma Janosko

Lupe Juarez

Charles Mohrle

**Architects**

ARCHITEXAS

Craig Melde

Gary Skotnicki

Richard Martratt

Jeff Cummings

David Chase

Elizabeth Cummings

Mark Scruggs

Jay Firsching, Preservation Specialist

**ANDRES CONSTRUCTION SERVICES, INC.**

Wade Andres

Jeff Kempf

Skipper Good

Kurt Dobson

Don Kloberdanz

Russell Finley

Keith Hanspard

**CARILLON**

Royal Eijsbouts Bell Foundry

Yost Eijsbouts

Joep Vanbrussell

**Carilloneur**

Gert Oldenbeuving

**Photos**

Andy Hanson

Dallas Morning News

Diocese of Dallas Archives

Diocese of Dallas Liturgy Office

Frantisek Zvardon

Skipper Good

Steve Landregan

Texas Catholic Newspaper

## CATHEDRAL GALA COMMITTEE

Raymond D. Nasher, Honorary Chairman

Dona & Reuben Martinez, Co-Chairs

Christy & Stewart Frazer, Co-Chairs

Marilyn & Jim Augur

Robert Baillargeon

Ms. Patricia Cowlishaw

Miriam Ackels Claerhout

Mrs. Suzanne Settle Dees

Jerry Hoag

Carole & John Ridings Lee, Jr.

Brenda McCord

Kelley McDonald

Neil O'Brien

Pat Porter

Ms. Lynn Haire Smith

Kip Tindell

Eugene Vilfordi

Tucean Webb

Lucy Witte

## Cathedral Gala Advisory Council

Jean & James Barrow

Mary & John Beecherl

Dr. Fred Bronstein, President

Peggy & Charles Galvin

Charles Gummer

Bette & Jerry Hoag

Mrs. Caroline Rose Hunt

Carol and Dr. Francis Lazarus

Mary & Tom Lazo, Sr.

Mickey & Bill Lively

Norma & Harry Longwell

Sarah & David Martineau

Janis & Dr. William Miles

Joyce & Harvey Mitchell

James M. Moroney, JR

Maria & Al Niemi

Erle Nye

Judy & Bill Pittman

Frank Ribelin

Deacon & Mrs. Denis Simon

Susan & Robert Sulentic

Peggy & Jere Thompson

Joy & Tom Wunderlick